Music Education in Your Hands

Music Education in Your Hands is a textbook for the introductory course in Music Education. Written for future classroom music teachers, the book provides an overview of the music education system, illuminating the many topics that music educators need to know, including technology, teaching methods, curricular evolution, legislation, and a range of societal needs from cultural diversity to evolving tastes in music. It encompasses a broad picture of the profession, and how the future of music education rests in the hands of today's student teachers as they learn how to become advocates for music in our schools.

FEATURES

- A balance of sound historical foundations with recent research and thinking;
- Coursework that is appropriate in level and length for a one semester introductory course;
- Actual dialogue between undergraduate music education majors and teachers, illustrating pertinent issues teachers must face;
- An emphasis on opportunities in the greater community beyond the walls of the school that music teachers should be familiar with;
- Suggested topics for activities and critical thinking for every chapter;
- A companion website including student and instructor resources

Michael L. Mark is the author of several music education books in the area of music education history. He is retired from Towson University, where he was Dean of the Graduate School and Professor of Music. A member of the Music Educators Hall of Fame, he is a frequent speaker at universities and symposia.

Patrice Madura is a Professor of Music Education at the Indiana University Jacobs School of Music, where she teaches freshmen through to doctoral students. She is the author of *Becoming a Choral Music Teacher*, and *Getting Started with Vocal Improvisation*, and of articles in *Teaching Music in the Urban Classroom*, *Journal of Research in Music Education*, *Bulletin of the Council for Research in Music Education*, and *International Journal of Music Education*, as well as many more publications.

Music Education in Your Hands

An Introduction for

Future Teachers

MICHAEL L. MARK
TOWSON UNIVERSITY
AND
PATRICE MADURA
INDIANA UNIVERSITY

Routledge
Taylor & Francis Group
NEW YORK AND LONDON

First published 2010
by Routledge
711 Third Avenue, New York, NY 10017

Simultaneously published in the UK
by Routledge
2 Park Square, Milton Park, Abingdon, Oxon OX14 4RN

Routledge is an imprint of the Taylor & Francis Group, an informa business

© 2010 Taylor & Francis

Typeset in Sabon and Neue Helvetica by Book Now Ltd, London

Library of Congress Cataloging in Publication Data
Mark, Michael L.
Music education in your hands: an introduction for future teachers / Michael L. Mark and Patrice Madura.
   p. cm.
Includes bibliographical references and index.
1. Music—Instruction and study—United States 2. School music—Instruction and study—United States I. Madura, Patrice D. II. Title.

MT3.U5M327 2010
780.71—dc22   2009024033

ISBN10: 0-415-80089-7 (hbk)
ISBN10: 0-415-80090-0 (pbk)
ISBN10: 0-203-86347-X (ebk)

ISBN13: 978-0-415-80089-1 (hbk)
ISBN13: 978-0-415-80090-7 (pbk)
ISBN13: 978-0-203-86347-3 (ebk)

Contents

Illustrations

Figures

Table

Preface

Sempre Avanti—
Always Forward

Change. Change happens. It is inevitable. Change is one of the major characteristics of modern society and we have no choice but to adjust and find ways to use it to our benefit. Music teachers continually adjust and adapt to change as it affects their profession in many ways. Often, they even influence and guide it. But there is also a constant in the lives of music educators: they must maintain the integrity of the music they teach and they must offer the highest possible quality of instruction as they keep up with technological, economic, and political changes that continually influence the schools and the processes of education.

This dialogue between two veteran music teachers is an example of music teachers' responses to change. Any new music educator can easily find a veteran teacher who would comfortably fit in this conversation.

Music Teacher A   I remember when I was a new teacher. Thirty-five years ago we pretty much relied on ourselves to do things that technology does now. Our most advanced "audio-visual" equipment was tape decks, stereo record players, and slide projectors. We wrote out music by hand, we charted the marching band with paper and pencil, we kept track of our music library on index cards and we played "drop the needle" on long playing vinyl records. We were just beginning to use synthesizers and we taught electronic music with them. But we didn't know that a flood of new technology was going to wash over our profession in the next few years.

Music Teacher B   Right—we didn't know what was coming! A lot has changed and the job of teaching music is different from what it was then. When I was an undergraduate, Kodály, Orff and Dalcroze approaches hadn't yet become popular in American education, and quality choral music for middle school students with changing voices was in much shorter supply than it is today. And as you say, it's been a challenge to stay on top of the technology of notation software, PowerPoint presentations, and digital recording, not to mention iPods, YouTube, and all the devices that are part of students' lives today. Things were simpler 25 years ago. But we have to keep up with the changing times if we want to be relevant to our students. Fortunately, my students enjoy teaching *me* about the latest technology and about their favorite songs. They help me stay current.

The authors recognize in this book that while teaching music is a dream job for many musicians, there are also negatives that must be recognized and challenges yet to be met. We discuss historical events that have informed music education practices as well as current political and demographic changes and advances in technology. Today's freshmen and sophomores need to understand the foundations, current practices, and future challenges that are part of our profession in order to prepare them to be effective participants and leaders, and to have active, satisfying careers as they enrich the lives of their students.

To the Professor

Music Education in Your Hands is a text for the freshman or sophomore course often called "Introduction to Music Education." Why still another text for the young music education student when there are already satisfactory books available? Our intention was to create a book that differs from currently available texts by:

- presenting a balance of sound historical foundations with cutting edge research and thinking;
- providing content that is appropriate in level and length for an introductory course;
- assisting both the instructor and the student with mastery of course topics through web-based quizzes, glossaries and other teaching materials.

Music Education in Your Hands is meant to prepare students for the music education courses they will take next—the variety of methods courses that build on the foundational knowledge presented in this book. The book presents an overview of the music education profession that illuminates the many changes that music educators need to know about—technology, teaching methods, curricular evolution, legislation, and a range of societal needs from cultural diversity to evolving tastes in music. *Music Education in Your Hands* is not a how-to-do-it book. Rather, it encompasses a broad picture of the profession, from why music education exists in schools to a look at what the future may bring.

We present much of the material in the form of dialogue between undergraduate music education majors, or between an experienced teacher and a future teacher. These transcriptions of actual conversations present material in an interesting manner that students can easily relate to. We also emphasize opportunities in the greater community beyond the walls of the school that music teachers should be familiar with.

Music Education in Your Hands includes a website that is continually updated. Every chapter ends with a list of suggested topics for activities and critical thinking about the chapter, and a bibliography. Its 11 chapters fit a one semester course comfortably. We suggest that it be used sequentially, although you might wish to shuffle some of the chapters to meet your particular requirements.

To the Student

Welcome to your first course in music education foundations. In this book you will encounter the historical foundations of the profession of music education, current approaches to teaching all levels and courses of public school music, and provocative questions about the future of music education. You will actively explore each of these topics through engaging chapter activities, where you will reflect on your own personal music education and compare and contrast it with various models for teaching. The book and its website provide you with quiz questions for practice and comprehension, as well as many resources for topics you would like to know more about.

Each chapter contains actual dialogue among students who, like you, are enrolled in an introductory course in music education. You will find that these dialogues help orient you to the course topics in an inviting and relevant way. You will probably have similar conversations with your peers and with your professors during the course of this semester. As you begin Chapter 1, you will read why other students want to be music teachers, and you can add your voice to their statements.

The purpose of our book is two-fold: to introduce you to a comprehensive view of music education that will prepare you for future coursework in teaching techniques and methods, and to present a realistic view of the life of a music teacher, so that you will be able to make informed decisions about your chosen career path. We hope you enjoy our book and that it inspires you to become the best music teacher you can be.

Acknowledgments

We thank the many friends and colleagues who assisted us as we completed this book: John Ceschini, executive director of Arts Education in Maryland Schools (AEMS), and Janice Webber, AEMS program director; Barbara King, consultant to the Maryland State Department of Education and former coordinator of music for the Howard County, Maryland Public Schools; Mary Ellen Cohn, executive director of the Maryland Music Educators Association; James Quinn; Dr. Estelle Jorgensen, professor of music education, Indiana University; IU undergraduates Tonya Mitchell and Nick Waldron whose dialogue and photographs throughout this book befriend them to the reader; the IU freshmen who provided valuable feedback during the trial semester of this book: Elizabeth Kent, Julian Morris, Hannah Dettmer, Kielty Wintersteen, Lee Anderson, Scott Gillespie, Elizabeth Duff, Zachary Brumbaugh, Vinéecia Buchanan, Kyanne Eisenhour; to the IU students and to the following individuals who allowed me (Patrice Madura) to photograph their musicians: Drs. Lissa May (and Christin Reardon) of IU Young Winds, Brent Gault of the IU Children's Choir, Katherine Strand of the IU xiv Preface

International Vocal Ensemble and Kwesi Brown of the African Drum and Dance Ensemble, Brenda Brenner of the IU Fairview Project, Beth Hayes of the University of New Orleans, and Kimberly Mercurio of Hinsdale, IL; Alain Barker, Director of Marketing and Publicity for the I.U. Jacobs School of Music; Linda Bucklin, Administrative Secretary of the IU Music Education Department; Richard Granlund, Patricia Wiehe and Craig Ghormley of North Central High School in Indianapolis, IN; Rebecca Cohen, MD; to the Routledge editorial staff, especially Constance Ditzel, Denny Tek, Nicole Solano, Sarah Stone and the outstanding editors and reviewers of the manuscript whose knowledgeable and wise suggestions have made this a better book than it would have been otherwise; and last but with the greatest thanks to our wonderful spouses, Lois and David, whose love and support mean everything.

Michael L. Mark
Baltimore, Maryland

Patrice Madura Ward-Steinman
Bloomington, Indiana

one
Why Music Education?

FIGURE 1.1 Tonya and Nick, Freshman Music Education majors

On the first day of the Introduction to Music Education course, Professor Jenkins asked the students why they want to be music teachers. This is what they said:

Nick　　　　　Playing in my high school band was meaningful to me in several ways. The concerts, the marching shows, and working together as a team to create music that everyone enjoyed were great experiences.

My band director was my inspiration to major in music education and I want to be a band director like him.

Tonya   After I started playing clarinet in seventh grade I got hooked on band like you did, Nick. I get so much enjoyment and satisfaction every time I perform. Even though I feel this way, I know most other band members won't major in music in college. I want to learn more about what motivates them to be in the high school music program.

Julian   My goal as a music educator isn't to inspire every student to become a *professional* musician. I want to inspire *every* student to keep music in their lives *always*. I hope all of my students will see music as a way of expressing themselves, as an outlet for emotion, and as a creative way to have fun!

Elizabeth   I want to be a music teacher because I think it's a very *meaningful* thing that I can do for my profession. I *love* music and I think it's a really important thing for kids who might not know what to do or what path they might go down. If I can give them a little guidance or at the very least a little enrichment to help them, then I think that's a very meaningful thing to do.

Lee   The teacher who made music click for me was a violist whom I had heard of before because my sister had taken violin lessons from him. I then heard he was going to be teaching at a music camp over the summer, which intrigued me. Right from the start of my lessons I knew things we're going to be great, because he told me this: "Lee, if you give me the chance and follow all of my instruction, I promise you that I can make you that much of a better player." He gave me the building blocks to playing viola that I had never received before, and with that I was able to incorporate my own thoughts into my playing. Ever since then I've wanted to become a music educator.

Kielty   I've always loved music and helping people is probably the one thing that gives me the most joy in the world and so a career where I can combine helping people and music makes it pretty obvious that teaching music is the only choice for me.

Vinéecia   For a long time I didn't know what my calling was in life, but recently I've discovered that teaching is something that I feel like I'm meant to do and music is something that's a really big part of me. Combining those two things is really exciting for me. I'd like to teach music to young children.

Zac   I had a great experience in band and it was my favorite thing about high school. I grew a lot during that time. My teacher really inspired me and I want to inspire kids that way to not only grow musically but to grow in other aspects of their life.

Kyanne   I want to be a music teacher so I can inspire kids the way my music teacher inspired me. She made me want to learn and to become a better person. High school band also gave me lots of experience working with younger kids. I really enjoy working with people in music.

Beth	I want to be a music teacher because I've always had a passion for music and I want music to stay in my life and teaching it would be the best way to do it.
Scott	I want to be a music teacher because choir is the one thing that I've truly felt a passion for and I want to share that with as many people as possible.
Hannah	I want to teach music because I want to share my passion for music and to make a difference in people's lives, and I think music teaching would be the best way to do it.
Professor Jenkins	There's a lot to know about why music affects people the way it does and why so many people want to participate in it. There's something unique about music that transforms people; that makes it important enough to justify it as a school subject. Think of your own experiences and how music has affected your lives. And people also value the effect that music has on schools and communities, not just the individuals. It even influences the culture of the entire country. These things help make music an important subject. As you prepare to be a music teacher, ask yourself this question: **Why is music education so important that I want to spend my entire professional life in it?**

What difference has music made in your life? Why do you want to teach it to children and young adults? What is it that attracts you—the opportunity to influence students' lives through music? Self-satisfaction? Being involved in the music itself? The chance to build a music program that reflects your personality and musical taste? These, and many other reasons, motivate music teachers. One or all of them might apply to you and you can probably come up with other reasons that you can verbalize at this point in your education.

History of Music Education

Music education is a proud and historic profession whose beginnings go back thousands of years. There has been music for as long as there have been civilizations, and there has been music education for as long as there has been music. Music education has always been part of the education systems that societies have created so their cultures can continue from one generation to the next.

From ancient times to the present, people have learned to sing, play instruments, dance, and create music, regardless of when and where they live. Every society throughout history has valued music and music teachers.

Music became a curricular, tax-supported subject in American public schools in 1838. The country was still young then, when Lowell Mason, a composer and teacher, convinced the Boston School Committee (Board of Education) that music needed to be included in the curriculum. At that time, the school music program consisted of vocal music. Students learned to read music and sing, and this pattern continued throughout the 19th century. It was only in the 20th century that instrumental music became commonplace in schools. Mason's contributions to American music extend beyond music in the schools. His hymns are still sung in churches and his teacher training methods prepared new music teachers throughout much of the 19th century. After that fateful year, 1838, music education gradually spread to schools throughout the entire country.

When we think about the role of music in education, we can take pride in its long and impressive history in meeting the musical needs of the nation. The United States has changed a great deal since Mason's time, and music education has continually evolved to meet the ever changing needs of the country.

Why does music have an important place in the curriculum? There are many reasons, mostly having to do with the nature of music and its relationship to society. Some of the great figures in Western history were eloquent on the subject. The Greek Philosopher Plato (427–347 BC) wrote: "Education in music is most sovereign, because more than anything else rhythm and harmony find their way to the inmost soul and take stronger hold upon it" (Mark 2008b, 5). Martin Luther (1483–1546), creator of the religious rebellion that spawned Protestantism, treasured the role of music in the church: "It was not without reason that the fathers and prophets wanted nothing else to be associated as closely with the Word of God as music" (Mark 2008b, 36).

One of the major figures in the growth of music education in the 20th century was Frances Elliott Clark. Clark was one of the founders of the Music Supervisors National Conference, later known as the Music Educators National Conference (it has since been renamed MENC: The National Association for Music Education). She wrote in 1919:

> The hour of music education has struck. Not music for fun nor entertainment, not as a pastime or accomplishment, nor yet as an art, standing alone—although at times it may be all of these—but as one of the great vital forces of education.

A more contemporary view agrees with Ms. Clark. The superintendent of a large city school system, like most superintendents, values music in his schools:

> I walk into so many schools where something hits me that tells me this place is alive. First it's the kids: they are happy. I have a conversation with a child or a teacher, and right away you get a sense of what's available, whether there is a choir or a band. There is generally a correlation between how rich are those conversations and how a school is doing. (Alonso 2008, 9)

Music Becomes a Curricular Subject

In 1838, when the Boston School Committee became the first in the United States to approve music in the public schools as a curricular, tax-supported subject, it was done in the belief that music was good for children physically, morally, and intellectually. Soon after, and continuing well into the 20th century, boards of education throughout the country adopted music as a curricular subject on the basis of that same three-part justification. It is interesting to look back at the justification through the eyes of 21st century music educators. Remarkably, it reflects contemporary thought about the role of music in education.

- **Music is good for children physically**—moving to music, exercising the body, fingers, breath control, vocal cords and lungs—all of these physical actions help us develop coordination of our large and small muscles, and control of our bodies.
- **Music is good for children intellectually**—this has become a familiar theme not only to music teachers, but to the general public as well. Numerous studies have shown relationships between music education and achievement in other academic subjects. We still do not know conclusively that music education causes students to achieve more. But the correlations indicate that music students achieve at higher levels and have higher graduation rates than those who do not study music or participate in it (http://www.menc.org/resources/view/academic-achievement-and-music).
- **Music is good for children morally**—here, the Boston School Committee was referring to music as a means of making students more positive, more considerate of each other, better team members, as well as other behaviors that affect their everyday lives and their attitudes toward school.

These reasons support music education to this day. The Boston School Committee showed extraordinary foresight in justifying music on the basis of these three criteria.

Philosophy of Music Education

Philosophy is the systematic study of such fundamental matters as existence, knowledge, truth, justice, beauty, mind, and language. A statement of philosophy in regard to music education is a statement of one's foundational belief. Many philosophers have explored and described the meaning of music and the importance of its expressive effect on people, as well as the benefits of music education as it meets the needs of their societies. Some music educators have studied the academic discipline of philosophy (which translated from Greek means "the love of wisdom") to help them understand the nature of music. They have written extensively and have theorized about music and its role in education.

One of the most influential philosophers is Bennett Reimer of Northwestern University, whose landmark book, *A Philosophy of Music Education*, was first published in 1970. That book emphasized the feelingful response to music as the primary purpose of music education. The feelings stimulated by music (the aesthetic response) led him to develop a philosophy called "Music Education as Aesthetic Education." Aesthetic education became the unifying philosophy of the music education profession throughout the country.

Reimer stated that music should be taught to children in an authentic, comprehensive manner, as opposed to devices like arranging music of various cultures to sound like Western music. This loses the authentic characteristics and meaning of the music and defeats the purpose of teaching the musics of other cultures. Learning the music of one's own culture, as well as that of others, allows students to understand themselves and their relationship to other cultures. Reimer was one of the authors of the basal series,

2004–2008	→	MENC National Anthem Project
2006	→	Centennial Symposium, "Centennial Declaration"
2003	→	Estelle Jorgensen publishes *Transforming Music Education*
2001	→	No Child Left Behind Act
2000	→	Goals 2000 Symposium, "The Housewright Declaration"
1995	→	David Elliott publishes *Music Matters*
1994	→	National Standards for Arts Education
1980–	→	Howard Gardner proposes music as one of seven intelligences
1974	→	MENC publishes *The School Music Program: Description and Standards*
1971	→	First National Assessment of Educational Progress in music
1970s	→	Piaget's developmental psychology influences American education
		MENC develops music education advocacy program
1970	→	Bennett Reimer publishes *A Philosophy of Music Education*
1969	→	The Goals and Objectives Project
1967	→	Tanglewood Symposium, "The Tanglewood Declaration"
1963–1973	→	Contemporary Music Project
1963	→	Yale Seminar
1960	→	Jerome Bruner publishes *The Process of Education*
1958–1963	→	Suzuki, Orff, Kodály methods come to the United States
1953	→	Allen Britton founds *Journal of Research in Music Education*
1950s–	→	Federal government becomes deeply involved in American schools
1934	→	Music Supervisors National Conference becomes Music Educators National Conference
1930s–	→	James Mursell, psychologist, influences music education
		Beginning of education reform movement that still exists
1910–1920	→	Frances Elliott Clark promotes phonograph in classroom music instruction
1907	→	Beginning of Music Supervisors National Conference
1900–	→	Émile Jaques-Dalcroze creates Eurhythmics
1837	→	Lowell Mason successfully advocates for music education as a tax-supported curricular subject
1780–1825	→	Johann Heinrich Pestalozzi's theories influence education
1746–1800	→	William Billings' colonial New England Yankee composer and singing school master
15th c.	→	Martin Luther advocates music education
11th c.	→	Guido d'Arezzo—beginning of music notation
6th c.	→	Boethius writes *De Musica*, text used almost a thousand years
4th–3rd c. BC	→	Plato, Aristotle praise music education

FIGURE 1.2 **Music education history timeline**

Silver Burdett Music, in which the presentation of music to children was based on the philosophy of aesthetic education.

There were other manifestations of aesthetic education as well, especially in the Comprehensive Musicianship (Mark 1996, 162) movement that began in the late 1960s and continues to this day in a variety of forms. Comprehensive Musicianship teaches several aspects of music through composition and performance. Rather than simply rehearsing and performing specific pieces, the student learns those pieces through an integrated approach combining music theory, history, and performance practices, including improvisation and world music. The rehearsal is the basis of a comprehensive music education, rather than a mechanistic approach to performance.

The Manhattanville Curriculum (named for Manhattanville College, where it originated) was a different approach to comprehensive musicianship. It used the "spiral curriculum," in which musical concepts were repeated several times over a period of time. With each repeat, the concepts became more advanced and refined (Mark 1996, 156).

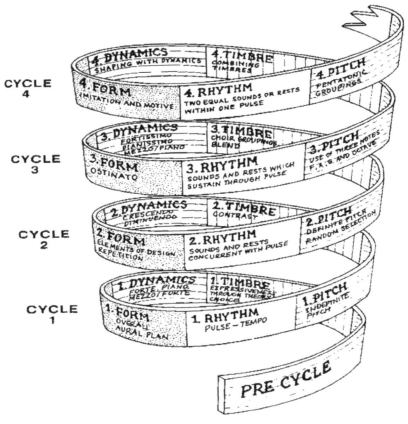

Note: Ronald B. Thomas, MMCP Final Report, Part 1 Abstract (United States Office of Education, ED 045 865, August 1970), pp. 39–49.

FIGURE 1.3 **Manhattanville Music Curriculum Project (MMCP) Curriculum Concept Spiral**

Another philosopher, David Elliott of New York University, wrote a book titled *Music Matters* (Elliott 1995), in which he proposed a new philosophy called praxialism. The term "praxial" originated in the Greek philosopher Aristotle's idea of *praxis*, which means action based on practice, rather than theory. The praxial philosophy describes music as action-based study of music, for which Elliott uses the word "musicing." Musicing includes performing, listening, composing, arranging, conducting, and creating. The focus is not on the work of art itself, as in music as aesthetic education, but on what one experiences when engaged in making music. Musicing helps students gain self-knowledge, growth, and self-esteem. These benefits affirm the value of music education in every culture. Praxial philosophers emphasize the need for students to experience music of both Western and non-Western cultures. In practice, the praxial philosophy emphasizes the roles that music plays in a variety of societies and the way that the people of those societies respond to their musics (McCarthy & Goble 2002, 19–26).

Philosopher Estelle Jorgensen of Indiana University defines music education more broadly. She proposes a humane and inclusive view of music education and the need for systemic change in practices. She recommends guiding principles for music teachers that bring together philosophy and the practice of music education (Jorgensen 1997, 2003, 2008).

We have touched briefly on profession-wide philosophies advocated by some of the intellectual leaders of the music education profession. But every individual music educator also has foundational beliefs about her work, and their unique views might not coincide with the philosophies discussed above. This is not unusual. In fact, it is healthy for the individual to continually ask why things are as they are in the profession, and to arrive at her own answers. Students preparing to be music teachers need a philosophical basis for their work.

Again, the music education student will have a philosophy of music education when she can answer this question: **Why is music education so important that I want to spend my entire professional life in it?** She might not have a deeply felt answer right now, but she should keep the question in mind as she proceeds through her college career and becomes a teacher. Eventually, she will come up with several reasons that might range from music education as entertainment for the school and community to the belief that music will influence her students positively throughout their lives.

Students should ask teachers the question. They should ask their professors and music education majors who have completed their student teaching. When she arrives at a belief that will support her work and can articulate it, she will be able to verbalize the reasons for what she does as a music educator. That will help her as she plans her curriculum, selects materials and establishes teaching methods, and as she discusses her program with administrators, parents, and the community.

Sociology and Multiculturalism

Sociology is the study of society and social relationships, organization, and change. For music educators, it means the study of the role of music education in contemporary society. Looking at society as a sociologist does, we see a complex mixture of cultures, generations, technological innovations, and rapid advancements in practically all things American, including music.

Musical Cultures

We live in a multicultural nation that is built on the labor and beliefs of people from virtually every country. The multitude of American traditions makes up the comprehensive culture of the United States, one of the most culturally diverse nations in the world. Schools serve the children of all of these traditions, and music teachers need to recognize the many cultural backgrounds of their students. Successful music educators are knowledgeable of the music of as many of the cultures that make up American society as possible. Not just the music of many cultures, but the role of that music in each distinct culture. African Americans, Latinos, Eastern Europeans, Asians, Native Americans, and Arabs are only a few of the cultures, and each group consists of many subcultures, most with their own musical traditions. This can be a challenge for music teachers, but one that enriches their lives as teachers and as musicians.

Technology

We are also members of a technological society, and music educators have benefitted greatly from the many hi-tech inventions that allow us to do our job better. In addition, we live in a fast-changing society where new inventions come out quickly and then are replaced in short order by newer ones. The pace of change affects music education in many ways, and music teachers need to remain continually aware of change so they will be in a position to keep up with current needs and practices.

Psychology

Psychology is the study of mental functioning and behavior. It is an important area of study for music educators because it helps us understand the mental processes associated with music learning, creativity, and performance. Some of the psychological theories that have affected music education are described here.

Psychologist Abraham Maslow proposed his theory of Humanism in the 1940s. He stated that students are "self-actualized" through the study of the arts, and that music can be taught best when instruction matches their level of maturity and attention (Rideout 2002, 35).

Behaviorism, promoted by Harvard psychologist B.F. Skinner in the 1950s and 1960s, said that all learning can be observed through students' behavior, and that external rewards and consequences motivate that behavior. Extrinsic motivators include such things as a contest medal or a star for completing an assignment (Rideout 2002, 33).

Cognitive psychology, on the other hand, recognizes that not all learning is observable, and it investigates mental processes like problem solving, memory, and language. This branch of psychology began to influence music education practices when Jerome Bruner wrote *The Process of Education* in 1960. His approach to the new cognitive psychology influenced the curriculum of every subject, including music (Rideout 2002, 35).

Another Harvard psychologist, Howard Gardner, theorized in his 1983 book, *Frames of Mind*, that people have seven discrete intelligences in differing amounts: musical, linguistic, logical-mathematical, spatial, bodily-kinesthetic, intrapersonal, and interpersonal. If music is indeed one of seven ways of knowing, it is clearly justified as a curricular subject and it is obvious why music educators take so much interest in Gardner's influential work (Rideout 2002, 35).

A Biological Basis for Music Learning

Since the 1980s, psychologists have worked with neuroscientists to learn more about how the brain reacts to music and music making. With the assistance of sophisticated technology, it is possible to see how different areas of the brain react in particular situations. Using functional magnetic resonance imaging to scan the brain, scientists have found that musicians' brains are different from those of non-musicians. Musicians have more gray matter, which is the part of the brain that processes information, and there are other differences as well. The work of psychologist Frances Rauscher (Rauscher 1996) and music educator Donald G. Campbell (Campbell 2007) suggests that certain musical experiences promote changes in the brain that could lead to greater academic achievement. Dr. Charles Limb found that musicians hear music differently from non-musicians, which means that musical training might affect the architecture of the brain (Limb 2008). This raises the question of whether these differences are inherited or if the brain changes as a result of musical experiences. If musical experiences are the cause, then the implications for music education are great because there would be physical evidence of how music affects people.

More advanced music education courses will cover the work of philosophers, psychologists, sociologists, and historians as they describe in greater detail those facets of music education that they have influenced.

Why Musicians Become Teachers

FIGURE 1.4 **New teachers discuss their experiences**

The Seminar

The Music Education Department holds a seminar for its students during each spring semester. Graduates return to their alma mater to take part in a panel discussion to talk about their work and their lives as music teachers. This year, three music teachers, all former music education students, participated. Ann Collins, a high school band director, graduated five years earlier. Eric Chan has been teaching middle school general music and chorus for three years. LaTisha Mitchell, an elementary instrumental and general music teacher, has been a music educator for 15 years. This is what they said:

Ann Collins   I didn't even think about what I wanted to do with my life until I began taking clarinet lessons in middle school. Everything clicked immediately. I was only a fair student and not a very good athlete, but when I began making music on the clarinet, I loved it. My teacher was encouraging, and I was in heaven when he told me I was ready to join the school band. He was patient and encouraging, but he was strict—if we didn't practice enough he let us know he was unhappy with our work. In high school I was first chair clarinet in the band and second in the orchestra. I learned a lot of interesting music that broadened my vision of good music. I took private lessons from a member of the symphony and improved enough to be sure that I wanted to play music for the rest of my life.

But when I entered college here, I got a surprise. I wasn't the best clarinetist any more. Several players were better. I didn't exactly become discouraged, but I realized that a career as a professional performer might not be in the cards for me. I began to think of other ways to earn a living in music, and my friends who were music education majors persuaded me to speak to Dr. Jenkins, the music education advisor. She told me some things about music teaching that interested me. Teaching itself is a kind of performance. The band and orchestra could be my instruments. If I did a good job, the students, my fellow teachers, parents, and even the community would appreciate what I was doing for the children.

Dr. Jenkins was right, although my band didn't get a very high rating in my first year and the orchestra did even poorer. But when I heard better groups from other schools I learned what had to be done. Our concerts got better, the marching band became more precise, and both the band and orchestra got 1 ratings in my second year. By the third year, the marching band had won a trophy and my principal got letters complimenting me for the excellent ensembles I had nurtured and built.

I'm proud of my record as a new teacher and am sure I want to do this for the rest of my career. I play in the community band and I'm the assistant conductor, so I get to work with adults too. I'm required to get a master's degree and I'll come back here for it. I don't know how I'll find the time, but the chair of the music department told me that classes are held at times when teachers can take them. Other people do it and so I can too. I'm looking forward to learning more about my profession.

Eric Chan   As a general music teacher and choral director, I teach kids to read music and to perform on keyboard instruments, in drumming circles and in singing groups. In my classes, we hear and perform classical music, jazz, and rock, and music of some of the Native American tribes, an African tribe, and various indigenous American musics. My students know enough about each culture to appreciate the role that music plays in those societies. About half of my students sing in the school chorus. I enjoy being able to switch from teaching music in a classroom to directing in a rehearsal room. We do four concerts a year and the parents and administrators tell me they enjoy hearing the chorus.

I like teaching, but to be perfectly honest, I don't love it. I just don't seem to have the passion and spark that other music teachers have. I know you'd like to hear nothing but praise for being a music teacher, but even though I like it, I don't get the deep satisfaction that I hear about from other music teachers. Sometimes I'm completely absorbed in what I'm doing. Other times, I'm not so sure it's what I want to do for the rest of my career. I think about the school principal's job and I wonder if I'd prefer to be in charge of a whole school like he is and to work with all the teachers, to have a budget to work with, to make decisions that affect everyone. Or maybe I'd like to do what my music supervisor does. But maybe I'm thinking too narrowly. Should I consider something like medical school? I'm conflicted—just not ready to settle down yet to a lifetime career. That's why I haven't begun my master's degree yet.

LaTisha Mitchell   Now that I've been in this game for 15 years I'm in it for good, for better or for worse. I love teaching kids, but I know the flip side of teaching too. Long hours of preparation, mediocre pay, classroom teachers who don't want to let pupils leave for class music lessons, etc., etc., etc. But when a kid produces those first sounds on an instrument that sound so bad to other people, it's music to me. If I keep him motivated I know what he's going to sound like in a month, six months, by the end of the school year. To me, nothing feels better than hearing them play at the end of the year, alone and in the beginners' band and orchestra. They're like little sponges who absorb everything and they love me for it. So do their parents. When I balance the good and the bad of teaching I don't even have to think about it. It's an easy choice.

My first music teacher was an enthusiastic and supportive person. The school had no rehearsal room and she taught in any room that was vacant at the time. She wrote out a lot of the music herself because there was no budget for it. But she always smiled and criticized us in a way that made us feel good, and we knew that we were making her happy. I wanted to be like her when I grew up and my path never changed through middle school, high school and college. I have a master's degree in music education, and I still play in a big band for the swing dance club. I love my life and wouldn't want to do any other kind of job.

What the Three Teachers Have Taught Us

The undergraduate students have a lot of information to digest from the three teachers. Two of the teachers are excited about their work. It fulfills them and they plan to continue teaching. They love their work and are satisfied and completed. Ann Collins is a relatively new teacher whose students have improved to the point where they perform demonstrably better in public appearances. She is excited to see so much growth and looks forward to her future as a teacher. She intends to continue maturing professionally and is motivated by the thought that her ensembles are going to get better and better because of her leadership.

The third teacher, LaTisha Mitchell, is a veteran music teacher who knows her profession in and out. She is very much aware of the negatives, but appreciates that the positives of her profession are worth everything to her. She is successful, loves children and teaching, and looks forward to many more years of teaching music. Her positive attitude is something that younger teachers should emulate as they navigate their way through the ups and downs of a teaching career.

The second teacher, Eric Chan, is a different story. He is successful but he might decide to change careers to find the right groove for his life. He has to make up his own mind, of course. Eric might continue teaching music and have a fulfilling, rewarding career. But he needs to be sure that he has the passion for music and for teaching that sustains successful teachers. He might decide to go into school administration or supervision. But excellent teachers expect complete dedication from their administrators and supervisors, and his lack of passion could easily become evident to the teachers he works with. If Eric decides to go to medical school, it is probably good for him and for the teaching and medical professions. He will have made an honest effort and come to a well-thought-out decision to seek a different career. In this way, music education is like every other profession—some people need to seek satisfaction by changing careers. It is a good thing. They avoid future frustration that can lead to burnout that is unhealthy for themselves and their pupils.

The speakers offered some good reasons for wanting to teach music, but there are many other reasons as well that need to be considered in preparing for a career in the music classroom. We will discover some of those reasons as we progress through this book.

Why Teach Music?

Teaching music offers many benefits to music teachers. On a strictly practical level, good teachers have a secure career, assuming that the economy doesn't force boards of education to reduce music programs. Teachers' salaries have increased to the point where they make a comfortable living, and the medical benefits and retirement plans in most places are excellent. A satisfying career in music education passes all too quickly, and a comfortable retirement is a wonderful reward for a career as a music teacher who makes wise use of retirement benefits.

Teachers and Students

Successful teachers are deeply interested in their students. They love music, and they love and respect young people. Many teachers are able to perform in the community while they work with kids in schools. They know students' needs and abilities at different ages so they can tailor their teaching to their pupils. They are proud when their kids respond to music knowledgeably, when they grow as musicians. Fulfilled teachers know how much they have done for their students. They know that they have made a positive contribution to their lives.

The Cultural Life of the Community

Music educators have the satisfaction of guiding students on the road to the richness of a music education. But they do much more than that. They contribute to the quality of life of their communities and the nation. MENC: The National Association for Music Education illustrates why teaching music can be so satisfying:

> Perhaps the basic reason that every child must have an education in music is that music is a part of the fabric of our society. The intrinsic value of music for each individual is widely recognized in the many cultures that make up American life—indeed, every human culture uses music to carry forward its ideas and ideals. The importance of music to our economy is without doubt. And the value of music in shaping individual abilities and character are evident ... Success in society ... is predicated on success in school.
>
> (see MENC, www.menc.org)

Summary

Future music teachers who want to know what to expect in their own careers should carefully analyze the words of the three music teachers who spoke to the undergraduate music education students. They need to prepare well, to become good musicians themselves, and to know effective techniques of teaching children of all ages. They can look forward to years of satisfying musical experiences while enriching the lives of generations of students.

Questions, Topics and Activities for Critical Thinking

1. What information has this chapter given you as you begin to answer the question: Why is music education important enough to spend my professional life in it?

2. List at least five reasons why you think that teaching music will be the right career for you.

3. Write a one-page essay about your future as a music teacher. What kind of teaching position do you want for your first job after you graduate? What long-term goals would you like to set? What professional and personal satisfaction will you expect to get from achieving those goals?

4. Do you agree with the three criteria that the Boston School Committee used? Why? Discuss why each of the three is or is not valid for today's music education.

5. Write a few paragraphs about whether your high school music program served all students (all races, creeds, religions, etc.) equally well. Were the ensembles that you performed in representative of the various cultures in your community? What music of your community's cultures did you perform in your ensembles?

6. What technology do you use now in your musical activities that did not exist five years ago?

7. Make a bibliography of at least six books about the psychology of music and/or music education that are in your school's music library.

Readings

Alonso, Andres (CEO of the Baltimore City Public School System, fall 2008). In *Peabody Magazine*. The Peabody Institute of The Johns Hopkins University.

Arts Education Partnership. Available http://aep-arts.org/.

Bruner, Jerome (1960). *The Process of Education*. New York: Harvard University Press.

Campbell, Donald G. (2007). *The Mozart Effect: Tapping the Power of Music to Heal the Body, Strengthen the Mind, and Unlock the Creative Spirit*. New York: Avon.

Campbell, Patricia Shehan (1996). *Music in Cultural Context: Eight Views on World Music Education*. Reston, VA: Music Educators National Conference.

Elliott, David L. (1995). *Music Matters: A New Philosophy of Music Education*. New York: Oxford University Press.

Gardner, Howard (1983). *Frames of Mind*. New York: Basic Books.

Jorgensen, Estelle R. (1997). *In Search of Music Education*. Urbana, IL: University of Illinois Press.

—— (2003). *Transforming Music Education*. Bloomington, IN: Indiana University Press.

—— (2008). *The Art of Teaching Music*. Bloomington, IN: Indiana University Press.

Limb, Charles (2008). "Music on the Mind." In *Hopkins Medicine*, also available http://www. hopkinsmedicine.org/hmn/s08/feature4.cfm.

Mark, Michael L. (1996). *Contemporary Music Education*, 3rd ed. New York: Schirmer Books.

—— (2008a). *A Concise History of American Music Education*. Lanham, MD: Rowman & Littlefield Education.

—— (2008b). *Music Education: Source Readings from Ancient Greece to Today*, 3rd ed. New York: Routledge.

McCarthy, Marie & Scott Goble (2002). "Music Education Philosophy: Changing Times." *Music Educators Journal*, 89, September, 19–26.

Music Educators Journal, September 2002 89. Articles on history, psychology, multiculturalism, technology, advocacy.

Peret, Isabelle & Robert J. Zatirre, eds. (2003). *The Cognitive Neuroscience of Music*. Oxford: Oxford University Press.

Rauscher, Frances (1996). "A Cognitive Basis for the Facilitation of Spatial-Temporal Cognition through Music Instruction." In *Ithaca Conference '96—Music as Intelligence: A Sourcebook*, ed. Verna Brummett (pp. 31–44). Ithaca, NY: Ithaca College.

Rauscher, Frances and Wilfried Gruhn (2007). *Neurosciences in Music Pedagogy*. Happauge, NY: Nova Science Publishers, Incorporated.

Reimer, Bennett (2003). *A Philosophy of Music Education: Advancing the Vision*, 3rd ed. Upper Saddle City, NJ: Prentice Hall.

Reimer, Bennett, Elizabeth Crook, Mary Hoffman, Albert McNeil, & David Walker (1974, 1978, 1981, 1985). *Silver Burdett Music*. Morristown, NJ: Silver Burdett Co.

Rideout, Roger (2002). "Psychology and Music Education since 1950." *Music Educators Journal, 89,* 33–37.

two
The Role of Government in School Music

Elizabeth tried to picture in her mind the school where she would have her first teaching job in a few years. She knew there is more to a school than teachers, students, and classrooms, but just what that "more" includes was beyond her because her school memories were limited to her own classes, rehearsals, and concerts. She knew that somebody is responsible for how schools are run, and that whoever makes those decisions must report to someone else who makes higher decisions. She wanted to know about these things and decided to ask Julian, her classmate, if he could answer some of her questions. This is their conversation:

Elizabeth   I'd like to know more about how schools are run and who makes all of the decisions. I'm wondering who decides how the budget is allocated and who organizes specific extra-curricular activities—whether that's the principals or the teachers in their respective schools. Do the parents have any say in what goes on in their children's district? And what's the role of the school board?

Julian   Those are really good questions. I know that from my experience, all the different tasks are delegated amongst a bunch of people. Not only do the teachers and the administrators have a say, but so do the parents and so do the students. At my high school we all congregated and made decisions as a whole, which is unique for a high school. But I think in any high school you're going to find that not all the decisions are made by the same person. It's usually a democratic process. But I don't know what kinds of decisions a school board makes.

Elizabeth   Well, I've been to a couple of school board meetings and I know that they hire and are ultimately responsible for letting teachers go. I also think that they have a role in deciding what extra-curricular activities are allowed and what ones aren't allowed. I know they also decide the dress code and other administrative things that a principal might differ on, so that they're kind of like the mediator. But as to their exact role, I think that's a good question we can ask Professor Jenkins in class.

FIGURE 2.1 **Professor addresses the class**

Dr. Jenkins OK—these are good questions, so today we'll have a civics lesson about how American democracy works. First of all, public schools are responsible to the public. The rules they live by are intended to make them as effective and valuable to their communities as possible so they can carry out their missions. There's no getting around rules. You could say that schools are like other public institutions such as hospitals and museums, for example. They're all responsible to the public and they have their own rules to follow. But this can be confusing because every school district in every state makes its own local rules—and there are about 13,000 school districts throughout the country. I wanted you to know the national scope so you'll see how complex it is. But if we get caught up in details here we'll lose the big picture, so for now let's take the broad view of how schools are run.

A Very Generalized Picture of the American Education Hierarchy

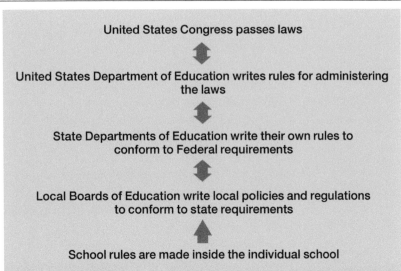

FIGURE 2.2 **A very generalized picture of the American education hierarchy**

Let's get back to the rules: some education rules come from inside the school and others from three different layers of government—local, state, and federal. Certain kinds of rules are made at each level that will affect you as a teacher in your everyday work. I'm talking about things like curriculum, buildings, salaries, and benefits. And are you surprised that I'm also talking about how many music books and keyboards and violas and saxophone reeds your school will buy in a particular year? How many music stands and spare guitar strings?

I'm sure you already know that the principal makes most of the rules that govern the everyday life of the students and teachers, counselors, cafeteria workers, volunteers and anyone else who works in the school. In some larger schools, the principal works with a council of department chairs and parent advisory groups. Sometimes, parents have enough authority to influence the principal about what teacher specialties to hire for her building, including music. What kinds of internal rules does the principal make that will affect you as a music teacher? Let me name just a few things: scheduling a rehearsal right after lunch when students are probably sleepy; deciding whether band members can miss a few days of school for a concert tour; allocating a few extra dollars to replenish instrument repair kits and replace strings and reeds; not assigning morning bus duty to the choir director so he can hold extra rehearsals before classes; deciding how much to charge for orchestra concert tickets and whether the orchestra gets to keep the money; how many concerts are performed during the school year; how involved the music performing groups

Elizabeth   will be in assemblies. And on and on and on. These might seem like mundane things, but they all affect the music program and any one of them could turn out to be a major issue for you as a music teacher. You'll learn quickly in your first teaching job how your own school is governed.

Elizabeth   I have another question. Who has power over the principal—who's the principal's boss? And does that person, or maybe it's the school board, really make a difference in the lives of music teachers?

Julian   Is it fair to say that the fate of a music teacher is divided up among the superintendent and the people who design the curriculum and people who are in control of the budget? Do they all have a say as far as what the music program will be like in a school?

Dr. Jenkins   Now we're talking about the superintendent and the board of education. The superintendent is the principal's boss, and he has a lot to do with music in schools. He has a boss too—the board of education—which appoints him. In fact, appointing the superintendent and overseeing his work are the board's most important responsibilities. The board of education represents the people of the school district in most communities, and it's responsible for the quality of education. It approves the school district's philosophy and the superintendent's plan of operation; it makes budget decisions for operating expenses and capital expenditures (buildings); and it's responsible for finance, curriculum and instruction, and personnel. In some states, local boards of education even set their communities' school tax rates. The board of education plays a key role in appointing new teachers. Even though the principals ordinarily hire their faculty, including music teachers, the process isn't complete until the board of education gives final approval and makes the appointments official.

The superintendent contributes experience, knowledge, and, hopefully, wisdom to help the board map out its strategy to achieve its goals. Most superintendents favor music education because they know how valuable their school music programs are. In case you're wondering how relevant the superintendent is to music teachers, a national survey found that six of the ten most powerful people in the country in arts education are superintendents of city school districts (Kessler 2008).

So much for local boards of education. Above them are the *state boards of education*. Almost every state, territory, and district in the country has a state board of education. The state boards set policy for curriculum, certifying teachers and administrators, and high school graduation requirements. They define the standards for "adequate yearly progress" in their own states (a requirement of the No Child Left Behind law), they coordinate statewide education planning, and they do a myriad of other things, including some that have a direct effect on music in the schools. Statewide fine arts standards are a good example. Most states require either one or one half a credit in the arts for graduation from high school. But some have no fine arts requirement.

Each state board oversees a state department of education, which is responsible for carrying out statewide school policies. Like local boards of education, one of the most important duties of state boards is to supervise the state superintendent of schools. The state superintendents carry a lot of weight in decisions about statewide support of music and other fine arts education. They make recommendations to the board for fine arts requirements, and most states have some version of fine arts expectations for all students.

Almost every state has fine arts standards that are approved by their boards of education. These standards are usually created by teams of fine arts teachers and administrators appointed by the board. The committee members who create them include teachers and administrators from many sections of the state, as well as community representatives like parents and professional consultants. The standards are usually released to the public for comments and reactions before the board gives them final approval.

State boards deal with other issues that affect music education too. For example, more than half of the states require students to pass high school exams in English, algebra, and science to graduate from high school. This often increases the time spent preparing for exams in those subjects and decreases the time students have for music.

Elizabeth	The state board of education seems to have a lot of power in allocating resources, so do they report to anybody or is that power contained among them and are they the highest level?
Dr. Jenkins	Both local and state boards of education ultimately are responsible to the public. They hold open meetings that the public attends, so citizens are aware of the board's vision, its work, and its effectiveness. Citizens expect high-quality education and they want responsible people to serve on school boards to make wise decisions about difficult issues. Most of their decisions involve money. It seems like there's never enough money, so they have to decide how to spend available funds for the best possible results in the schools. You know—how do they get "the most bang for the buck."
Elizabeth	It seems a little overwhelming that there are so many boards of education and superintendents and leaders making different decisions for different schools. And I'm wondering what would be the problem with having the education system be uniform in all of the states? Do you see a problem with having the same system for the whole country?
Julian	I think on some level we do have the same educational system in every state. Sure, there are differences but I think there are some very important similarities as well, because the federal government is on top of the state governments who control education. So I think what

the federal government does in terms of their role in education is to unify all of the states. But I agree that there are a lot of differences and sometimes it's confusing.

Dr. Jenkins   There's a reason for so many school districts, and the reason is the Constitution of the United States. The tenth amendment of the Constitution says that the states are responsible for any powers that aren't mentioned in the Constitution. Education isn't mentioned and so it's a state responsibility. That makes the states the highest authority in education, and that's why every state has its own state board of education and superintendent of schools, and why there are so many local school districts throughout the country.

Theoretically, the federal government isn't supposed to control what's taught in the schools, but it doesn't always work that way. When you pay your federal tax every year, the government returns some of that money to the states for specific uses. No state can afford to operate without that money. They couldn't afford to run their schools. They couldn't build roads or pay for all kinds of other public projects. So even though the federal government technically shouldn't be involved, it does indeed play a large part in controlling local curricula (Mark 2008). The best example I can think of is the *No Child Left Behind Act* of 2002. (NCLB is an amendment of the Elementary and Secondary Education Act of 1965. The numbering system of public laws identifies the Congress that passed the legislation and the number of the specific bill. NCLB is P.L. 107-110. It was the 107th bill to be passed into law by the 110th Congress.)

Even though education is the responsibility of the states, the federal government enforces NCLB by making it voluntary for the states. States can ignore it if they choose. But if a state should go that route, it would lose federal funds and wouldn't have enough money to operate. So naturally, all of the states have to conform to NCLB. A survey of music teachers about the effects of NCLB illuminates how it is viewed by the profession (http://www.menc.org/resources/view/no-child-left-behind-survey).

The Federal government expects each state to create minimum standards for reading, math, and science and to test for progress in those subjects. The arts are recognized as a core subject under NCLB, but schools aren't required to test for any subjects other than the three subjects. However, most states have standards for music education that guide teachers in designing curriculum, and some have even developed statewide music tests. No state requires a high school graduation examination in fine arts, although some that already have statewide music curricula are creating statewide tests. This is a contentious topic for ongoing consideration that needs a lot of attention if it is ever to become a reality. Music educators don't agree on whether statewide music testing would help music or hurt it. If

	students do well, then that would be helpful. But if teachers don't follow the statewide curriculum and their students do poorly on the test, it would reflect badly on music education. That could have severe implications for the music program.
Elizabeth	Does the *No Child Left Behind Act* affect music programs at all? What sorts of problems does it cause for music teachers?
Dr. Jenkins	It does cause problems, especially when time is taken from music programs to increase the amount of time given to the subjects that NCLB requires to be tested. Music teachers often have to find ways to adapt to less time for music instruction and rehearsals. One method that's beginning to find its way into American schools is integrating music into the general curriculum, so music teachers work with other teachers to enrich subjects other than music. Music is a natural in helping to teach science, math, and reading because it incorporates elements of these subjects. Music educators who help integrate music into the curriculum have to be sure that the purpose of music instruction doesn't become to support other subjects. Ideally, curriculum integration teaches music while it helps teach other subjects at the same time.

We have to take a positive approach and treat every problem as an opportunity that opens new doors for us. We've done this over and over throughout the last few decades. We've found ways to adapt to changing needs, which has allowed music to remain a strong member of the curriculum in most places.

Just to pick another issue out of the air, schools often change in other ways too. Let me give you an example: administrators always seem to be reconfiguring schools to help students become more effective learners. A lot of communities used to have large high schools, some with several thousand students. Now, educators believe that students do better in smaller schools where they know more people and where the teachers are more familiar with their students. It's not unusual for large high schools to be divided into two or more smaller schools that are sometimes called academies. A single high school building now might house separate academies that are schools in themselves. A single music program might serve more than one academy, or it might only serve one academy, which means there are fewer students for the music program. Also, some of the new smaller schools have a specific academic focus that are called "career academies," or "theme focused schools." Many focus on preparing students for work after graduation rather than for college. Or they might emphasize science, the arts, technology, or any other subject of particular interest to students. Regardless of the school's emphasis, there are likely to be students who want to be involved in music, but fewer resources might be available for music programs. There might not be as much time allocated to the music program, financial support could be less than in other schools, and the principal might tend to give more attention to the school's focus on subjects that are required to be tested.

Elizabeth   I didn't realize before this conversation and before I began studying music education that there's *so much* to know about schools before you get your first teaching position. But I guess I don't really have to worry about that yet. My main goal right now should be to be the best student that I can and learn as much about music education and music as I can to better myself and be the best teacher I can possibly be and be ready to address these issues when I enter my first teaching position.

Questions, Topics and Activities for Critical Thinking

1. Try to picture how music education would be different if there were a single unified national education system, rather than separate systems for each state. Would federal control have produced music education programs similar to what exists now? Would a nationwide curriculum serve our students and teachers better? Would teacher training programs be the same throughout the country?
2. Find out the ways in which your state board of education has affected music education in your state. You might get information from the officers of your state music education association or from the state board of education website.
3. Discuss the impact of the No Child Left Behind law on music education as you understand it. Look up your home state's NCLB evaluation to see if there is any mention of music or arts: http://www.ed.gov/nclb/landing.jhtml.
4. Should music be one of the tested subjects as part of No Child Left Behind, along with English, mathematics, and science? Why? If so, all of the public schools in every state would be judged on student performance on the tests. Would that be a good thing?
5. Are you aware of schools that have been divided into smaller schools, or academies? Try to learn what the effect has been on music instruction in those schools and share your findings with the class.

Readings

Arts Education in Public Elementary and Secondary Schools: 1999–2000. June 2000. Washington, DC: U.S. Department of Education Office of Educational Research and Improvement (NCES 2002–121).

Arts Education State Policy Database: 2007–2008 AEP. Available http://www.aep-arts.org/database/.

Education Commission of the States (November 2005). *State Notes: Arts in Education,* "State Policies Regarding Arts in Education." 700 Broadway, Suite 1200, Denver, CO 80203.

Isaacson, Walter (April 27, 2009). "How to Raise the Standard in America's Schools." *Time,* 32–36.

Kessler, Richard (August 28, 2008). "The 10 Most Powerful People in K–12 Arts Education." *Arts Education in the News.* The Dana Foundation, 3.

Mark, Michael L. (2008). *A Concise History of American Music Education.* Lanham, MD: Rowman & Littlefield Education, 174.

State standards for music education available:
   http://www.educationworld.com/standards/state/ct/index.shtml#fine
   http://www.educationworld.com/standards/state/toc/index.shtml#arts

three
The Music
Curriculum for
All Students

As Tonya and Nick walked to their Introduction to Music Education class they conversed about their homework reading assignment, which was general music in the schools. Their conversation went something like this:

Tonya	I just read that only 10–20% of high school students play or sing in school ensembles. So that means at least 80% of students don't take any music classes at all. I think there's something wrong with this picture.
Nick	Well, if they can't play or sing, then they can't take music class, right? We can't have non-musicians in our ensembles!
Tonya	Shouldn't all students be able to study some kind of music in high school? What about the people who want to learn to play an instrument or sing? Don't you think there should be music classes for people who don't want to be in band, orchestra or choir? Like maybe a guitar class—or a history of jazz class?
Nick	Well, if they never perform, where are they going to show us what they learned? When I think of music class, I think of someone getting on stage and performing. I never thought of general music class as a *real* music class. That's just sitting there learning about it. Music means playing and performing. In theory and history class you're not performing, you're just learning. Is it really a music class if you never perform for anyone?
Tonya	There's more to music than just performing. You don't have to be a performer to be a musician, or to appreciate music. It's still beneficial to those students whether they get to perform or not. Many students get left out. Everyone should have the chance to learn or appreciate music in any capacity that they want to. It should be for every student.

Nick	Now that you mention it, I remember that my friend took a beginning piano class at his high school. He loved it and still plays. You're right; there should be other music opportunities besides band, choir and orchestra so *every* student can learn music. And if more students study music in school, there'll be more people who support music all of their lives. We need interested and appreciative audiences for our concerts.
Tonya	Let's brainstorm about it. I'm thinking that if we really want to educate more students about other kinds of music besides choir, band and orchestra, we should start in the earlier grades. When I was in elementary school, all we did was sing songs once a week. Why shouldn't music be an exciting part of an elementary school education?
Nick	I was lucky—I had a great elementary school music experience. We had an Orff program and we played and improvised on recorders, xylophones and other percussion instruments. We created music from poems. That's the experience that made me decide to enroll in music in middle school.
Tonya	I wish I'd had a better school music program when I was small. My parents enrolled me in piano lessons in second grade, but a lot of kids can't afford private lessons. The only place they'd be able to learn music is in school.

I'd like to learn more about the Orff program. I wonder if there are other interesting ways to teach music to kids who aren't in instrumental or choral ensembles. I always thought that I wanted to direct high school ensembles, but now you've got me thinking about how great it would be to give *every* student a chance to learn music. |

Curriculum

Nick and Tonya have been discussing the music curriculum. "Curriculum" refers to the overall structure of courses and content that schools offer. Most music education majors think of their own high school ensemble experiences as the music curriculum, but Tonya is thinking more broadly and deeply. She is imagining a curriculum from the bottom up. Students who begin their musical development early in elementary school will probably have higher music aptitude and skill levels by the time they get to high school.

General Music

The term "general music" refers to the music classes that are designed for all students, not just for those involved in performance ensembles. General music classes are usually required for students in every elementary school grade. But when students reach middle school, the general music requirement is often reduced to a six- to nine-week class for sixth graders. Typically, there is no requirement for general music for seventh through twelfth grades. Many students never enroll in music electives, and only 10–20% of high school students participate in choir, band, and orchestra (Meske 1975; Siebenaler 2006; Digest of Education Statistics 2007). Elementary and secondary general music is an important consideration in planning curriculum.

Elementary General Music

The types of general music curricula offered in elementary schools vary widely, depending on the music teacher's training in elementary music methods. Some approaches are well defined, and others are an eclectic blend of the music teacher's areas of expertise. They all can be extraordinarily rich. Because early music study is so important to future music participation, and because music class is usually required in the elementary school, the most highly regarded approaches to teaching young children are described here.

FIGURE 3.1 **Singing children**

The Kodály Method

The Kodály method is named after the Hungarian composer Zoltán Kodály (1882–1967). Traditionally, Hungary was a musical country with a wonderful body of well-loved folk music. But Kodály became concerned because he saw his nation's musicality declining. The method that he created to restore Hungary's musical heritage focuses on music literacy. "Literacy" refers not only to the ability to read music well, but to understand it when listening, and to improvise and compose.

The Kodály method teaches children to become fully literate musicians, primarily through singing because the voice is the one instrument that every person owns. Zoltán

Kodály believed that children should be able to sing their folk songs and know the art music of their culture. His method is based on moveable "do" solfege (Do Re Mi Fa So La Ti Do), and Curwen hand signs to represent those solfege syllables.

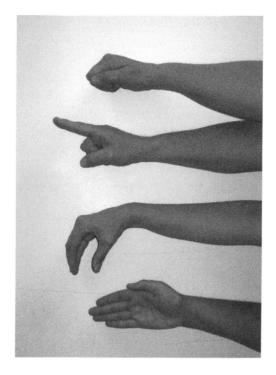

FIGURE 3.2
So La Ti Do

FIGURE 3.3
Curwen hand signs—
Do Re Mi Fa

Rhythm syllables, as developed by Émile Chevé, are used to represent rhythmic values:

Chevé Rhythm Syllables

"ta" for a quarter note
"ta-a" for a half note
"ta-a-a" for a dotted half note
"ta-a-a-a" for a whole note
"ti" for an eighth note
"ti-ti" for two eighth notes
"ta-i ti" for a dotted quarter note and eighth note
"ti-ri-ti-ri" for four sixteenth notes
"ti ti-ri"for an eighth followed by two sixteenth notes
"ti-ri ti" for two sixteenths followed by an eighth note

One of the most impressive aspects of the Kodály method is the finely sequenced curriculum for learning the concepts of pitch, rhythm, meter, and form, taught in three stages: preparation, presentation, and practice. In the preparation stage, the child experiences the concept as "sound before symbol," followed by the use of iconic symbols like pictures of familiar objects to represent beats. First grade students sing simple songs with limited vocal range (approximately middle C up to A) (Choksy 1999).

Hungarian children who are taught with the Kodály method become excellent music readers and musicians during their elementary school years. Simple staff notation is introduced in the second grade and by grade five students have been introduced to scales, modes and harmonies, and can improvise and compose with all musical elements and in all keys (Choksy 1999). By the time they complete high school, they can sight-sing even the most advanced atonal music.

A basic Kodály curriculum is provided below to illustrate the breadth of concepts to be learned during elementary school, assuming students have access to at least two 25-minute music lessons per week throughout the year.

Grade 1	Grade 2	Grade 3	Grade 4	Grade 5	Grade 6
Quarter note, Quarter rest, Eighth note, Half note	Half note, Dotted quarter	Whole note	Sixteenth notes, Dotted half notes	Dotted eighth note	
Beat, accent, Ostinato, 2/4 meter, Measure, Repeat	Ties, 6/8 and 4/4 meters, Fermata	Upbeat, Compound Duple meter	¾ meter	Augmentation, Diminution, Cut time, 9/8 & 12/8 meter	Mixed & unusual meters
So, mi, la	Do, re, so	Minor mode	Pentatonic scales, Fa, ti, Key signature	I & V Chords, Natural & harmonic minor	ii & V7 chords, Major, Dorian & Mixolydian modes

TABLE 3.1 **Kodály curriculum for introducing new rhythms and tonal concepts (Choksy 1999)**

The Kodály Method for American Children was developed by Katinka Skipiades Daniel with the approval of Zoltán Kodály. It was presented at the first International Kodály Conference, held in Oakland, California, in 1971. Kodály experts have created teaching materials, workshops, and teacher certification courses; and the Organization of American Kodály Educators (OAKE) and its publication, *The Kodály Envoy*, are notable for the strong influence they have had on music literacy in the United States.[1]

The Orff Approach

The Orff-Schulwerk was developed by German composers Carl Orff (1895–1982) and Gunild Keetman (1904–1990). This creative teaching "approach" (considered to be more loosely structured than a stricter "method") is based on "elemental" music. Elemental music refers to music that children make naturally, without training, and connects that natural music-making with fundamental movement and speech rhythms. The spirit of the Orff process embraces two key aspects: exploration and experience. As the child progresses, her music gradually becomes more refined. Rhythms are transferred from body movements to mallet percussion instruments in ostinati and drones, and later to pentatonic melodies.

FIGURE 3.4 **Orff instruments**

The Orff "instrumentarium" is a unique orchestra of diverse rhythm instruments, including drums, rattles, xylophones, metallophones, and glockenspiels, as well as recorders. These were inspired by Carl Orff's interest in the African xylophone and the Indonesian gamelan as "elemental" instruments (Choksy, et al. 2001). Students are active participants in ensemble performance, which requires attentive listening and physical coordination. Importantly, it also includes improvisation. The ensemble performance is often coordinated with a dramatic story or poem that is acted out or danced by other children in the class. *Orff Schulwerk: A "Simple Gift" to Music Education* is an outstanding videotape that features students in the Upper Nyack (NY) Elementary School under the direction of music teacher Judith Thomas, who demonstrates four stages of the Orff process: imitation, exploration, literacy, and improvisation.

The American Orff-Schulwerk Association (AOSA) is a vital professional organization that produces an array of teaching materials, workshops, levels of teacher certification, and a respected journal, *The Orff Echo*.[2] The AOSA's philosophy is that "music and movement—to speak, sing and play; to listen and understand; to move and create—should be an active and joyful experience."

The Dalcroze Approach

The Dalcroze approach is somewhat less well known than those of Kodály and Orff, but it is no less ingenious. When Émile Jaques-Dalcroze (1865–1950) was a young professor at the Geneva Conservatory in Switzerland, he was dissatisfied with the theoretical and fragmented ways in which music was taught. He sought to discover new ways to help his students develop their listening, expressive and rhythmic skills. He was inspired as he watched from his window one of his students walk with a perfect rhythmic gait, despite a poor sense of rhythm in the classroom. Thus, Eurhythmics, his approach to rhythm, phrasing, and expression through natural and attentive body movement, was born. Two other key components of the Dalcroze approach are the use of solfege, and improvisation; and these are always integrated with movement or gesture.

The Dalcroze approach is applicable to teaching music from early childhood through graduate school. Information on instruction for children, adults, and teachers can be found on the The Dalcroze Society of America's website,[3] and Virginia Mead's book, *Dalcroze Eurhythmics*, is another essential resource for music educators.

Although the essence of the Dalcroze approach cannot be learned in this short chapter, the following Eurhythmics activity will give a sense of the value of pursuing future coursework in this area. The teacher usually improvises at the piano for the class activity, as Dalcroze did, but recordings or class singing may be used as well.

The class should form two circles, one enclosed within the other. Any improvised piece, recording or song can be used, such as the Shaker tune, *Simple Gifts*:

'Tis a Gift to be Simple, 'Tis a Gift to be Free,
'Tis a Gift to Come Down Where you Ought to Be,
And When you Find Yourself in the Place Just Right
'Twill Be in the Valley of Love and Delight.

Step 1: The class steps to every beat on the first phrase, to every other beat on the second phrase, to the rhythm of the melody on the third phrase, and to the harmonic rhythm on the fourth phrase. For each phrase, the students also turn to face the opposite direction by the downbeat of the next phrase.

Step 2: The teacher will assign a number to each layer of rhythm performed above (1 for every beat, 2 for every other beat, 3 for melodic rhythm, and 4 for harmonic rhythm). The class steps to the four different layers of rhythm as above, but immediately on command by the teacher who will shout a number (1 through 4). The student must remember which layer the number refers to, and change movement and direction instantaneously which requires concentration, attention, and fast reaction time.

Step 3: The class designs a particular expressive movement for each layer of rhythm, and the two circles express different movements/layers simultaneously, but again cued by the teacher to immediately change movement whenever the word "change" is shouted, which may occur several times and when least expected.

Gordon's Music Learning Theory

The goal of Music Learning Theory is "audiation," a term coined by scholar-teacher Edwin E. Gordon for the ability to mentally hear written music notation when no sound is present. Gordon explains that he was more interested in "what … when … and why" rather than "how to teach" music (Gordon 1991, as cited in Mark 1996, 169). The resulting Music Learning Theory is well developed and includes a detailed approach to a combined sequence of skills, tonal patterns and rhythm patterns. These sequences of skill and pattern "vocabulary" are taught first through rote ("aural/oral" which includes imitation and singing, "verbal association" which includes labels or syllables for tonal/rhythmic patterns, and "partial synthesis" which includes hearing patterns as part of a whole rather than in isolation) in order to develop musical discrimination skills. A later step in discrimination learning involves musical symbols, enabling students to read and write the musical patterns that they hear (Mark 1996).

Following discrimination learning, Gordon's theory emphasizes inferential learning, in which the basic learned vocabulary of tonal and rhythmic patterns can be used by the student to discover new patterns, to creatively improvise with those patterns, and to understand music theory (Mark 1996). In order to improvise, Gordon (http://www.giml.org/mlt_applications.php#improv) prescribes the following sequence of steps:

1. Learn to sing several tunes by ear.
2. Learn tunes thoroughly and accurately.
3. Learn to sing the bass line, which is the foundation for understanding the harmony of a tune.
4. Use familiar tunes of appropriate difficulty.
5. Focus on the ear, rather than the written notes and theory.
6. Try to make up your own melodies.
7. Improvise with tonal and rhythm patterns.

For more information on Music Learning Theory, refer to Gordon's *Learning Sequences in Music: Skill, Content, and Patterns* or www.giml.org.

A Recommendation

There is much to gain through the study of the Kodály, Orff, Dalcroze and Gordon approaches, and it is strongly recommended that all music educators become familiar with them through coursework or workshops. They should also take extended study in at least one approach when time allows. The insights and strategies for developing student musicianship are unique, enlightening, and applicable to all teaching levels, including high school ensemble directing.

Other Approaches

Some elementary music teachers are specialists in the Kodály, Orff, or Gordon approaches, while others combine parts of these approaches or develop their own. Helpful resources exist for determining the scope and sequence of the elementary general music curriculum, including the basal series textbooks, *The National Standards for Arts Education* (1994) and the MENC website (www.menc.org).

No matter which method is used, the elementary general music curriculum should be designed to teach a sequential approach to the elements of music (melody, harmony, rhythm, form, texture and expressive qualities) through active skills (singing, playing instruments, reading, listening, improvising and composing), and sequenced according to the developmental capabilities of the child. For example, kindergartners learn basic concepts of melody (e.g., pitches can get higher) or rhythm (e.g., music has a steady beat) through singing, listening and moving to simple songs. Over time the concepts and skills become more and more advanced, so that by the fifth grade, students have internalized sophisticated knowledge of the concepts of melody, rhythm, harmony, texture, form, and expressive qualities through increasingly complex musical skills. This is an example of the Manhattanville Curriculum, which is illustrated in Chapter 1.

Continuing Teacher Development

Four or five years in a university music education program cannot teach a student everything she will need to know to be an effective teacher. Good teachers continually develop their skills throughout their professional lives. They attend conferences and workshops like those sponsored by the MENC-affiliated state associations and the Mountain Lake Colloquium for Teachers of General Music Methods. They read professional journals such as *General Music Today*, and books like *Songs in Their Heads: Music and Its Meaning in Children's Lives* (Campbell 1998).

Secondary General Music

"Secondary General Music" refers to music classes other than the traditional performance ensembles of choir, band and orchestra that are offered in middle schools and high schools. Advanced Placement (AP) Music Theory is one kind of secondary general music course, but there are many other possibilities that the music teacher can create based on her areas of expertise and student interest. Some examples of successful secondary general music courses that interest many students are piano, guitar, and music technology classes. Other courses might include world drumming, arts integration, playing the blues, recording arts, or the history of rock music. The possibilities are endless—they depend on the music teacher's creativity.

Piano Class

There is great value in offering piano classes at the high school level. Students with piano experience are often the strongest sight-readers (Demorest 2001), and the piano is the best visual instrument for teaching and understanding scales, intervals, and chords. These skills are essential for students who plan to pursue music at the college level. They enable students to be better all-around musicians. The piano is an orchestra in itself, capable of playing melodies, harmonies, bass lines and percussive accompaniments, making it a satisfying instrument to play throughout one's entire life, unlike a solo instrument that requires accompaniment.

The basic requirement for offering a piano class at the secondary school level is a keyboard laboratory, complete with electronic pianos and headphones for each keyboard. The keys need to be regulation-size piano keys and the action must be touch-sensitive like an acoustic piano. Beyond that, there are many sophisticated piano lab configurations complete with midi capabilities and software, but these are not necessary for a basic piano class.

Music education graduates should be capable of teaching a beginning piano class at the middle or high school level, and there are many beginning piano methods from which to choose, including Alfred's *Piano 101: Book 1* by Lancaster and Renfrow.

Guitar Class

The secondary general music class in guitar is popular for obvious reasons. It is a portable instrument that students can learn to play in a relatively short amount of time. With practice, most secondary students can master within a semester's time the three primary chords in the keys of G, D, and A major, and A minor along with simple melodic lines. Although most music education majors are required to demonstrate guitar proficiency in their elementary music education methods course, those students with guitar as their major instrument will most enjoy organizing and teaching a secondary general guitar class. As with teaching piano class, there are many beginning guitar method books to help structure the course. Requirements for a 20-student guitar class are 20 guitars with hard-shell cases, chairs, music stands, foot stands, replacement nylon strings, and a storage area.

World Music Drumming

World music drumming has found its way into school music programs due in part to a former president of MENC, Will Schmidt. He has published textbooks, complete with

FIGURE 3.5 **World Rock Ensemble**

DVDs and teachers' editions for the secondary general music classroom. *World Music Drumming* is a curriculum of 30 lessons divided into seven units, each of which culminates in an ensemble performance. In addition, the *Silver Burdett Making Music* (2008) textbook series features extensive world drumming units in grades 6, 7, and 8. These units include West African and Caribbean musical styles as well as Middle Eastern, Japanese, Native American, Brazilian, and many contemporary styles.[4] Watch for drum circle events and world music festivals in your area to experience drumming first hand, and to identify contacts and resources for your classroom.

Improvisation Ensembles

Another nontraditional music class is the free improvisation group that explores the sound environment and creates collaborative pieces beyond what is normally considered music. Improvised sounds include body percussion, finger snaps, claps, lip smacks, tongue clucks, whistles, whispers, and shouts, as well as "found sounds," which are any objects that can make interesting sounds. The class can improvise free form "soundscapes," such as a nature concert, a beach scene, or a crowded freeway; or create nontraditional "graphic" musical scores. Improvisers should always be guided to listen carefully and join in when they have "something to say," rather than artificially producing sounds with no aesthetic intent.

There are excellent textbooks and graphic scores for guiding the free improvisation ensemble. The quintessential textbook is *The Thinking Ear* (1988) by R. Murray Schafer, which provides the class with hundreds of ideas and lessons for "thinking outside the box," and is age-appropriate for middle school and high school students. It includes numerous poems and sketches for improvisatory interpretations. Another helpful resource designed specifically for voices is Patrice Madura's *Getting Started with Vocal Improvisation* (1999).

The International Society for Improvised Music (ISIM) is a professional organization that promotes performance, education, and research in improvisation.[5] Annual ISIM conferences feature concerts, lectures, workshops and materials. An extraordinary ground-breaking and enjoyable textbook is *Improvisation Games for Classical Musicians: 500+ Non-Jazz Games for Performers, Educators, and Everyone Else* by Jeffrey Agrell (2008). This book includes a course syllabus for an Introduction to Improvisation course for eight to sixteen students. The section devoted to the general music student includes warm-ups, drum circles, call and response games, body percussion and sound-painting (www.soundpainting.com).

Music Theory and Composition

Many high schools offer Advanced Placement (AP) Music Theory for students preparing to enter college as music majors. It is often taken by students who participate in one of the school's ensembles or in private lessons, and by students who are interested in composition. The course is organized to teach score analysis, aural analysis, sight-singing, dictation skills, piano skills, arranging and composition. The College Board and Educational Testing Service publishes a Teacher's Edition for the AP Theory class, which includes a clearly sequenced curriculum with sample yearly plans (http://apcentral. collegeboard.com/apc/public/courses/teachers_corner/2261.html).

Music Technology

Digital technology has changed the face of the AP Theory course, and today students (and teachers) are expected to use notation programs, sequencers, and digital keyboards. computer-aided instruction (CAI) is often used in addition to teacher instruction, which includes CD-ROM-based multimedia applications and multimedia authoring software. The Internet is also useful as a resource for classroom instruction, including distance learning, where classrooms can have live interaction with each other. The new teacher must prepare for changing technology by taking advantage of workshops, music technology journals like *Electronic Musician* and *Keyboard*, and organizations like the Association for Technology in Music Instruction[6] and The Society for Music Theory.[7] Other useful resources are *Why and How to Teach Music Composition*, edited by Maud Hickey (Hickey 2003), and *Experiencing Music Technology* by David Williams and Peter Webster (2009) (http://teachmusictech.com/emtbook/index.htm).

Music Appreciation and History

Classical music has traditionally been the focus of music appreciation courses to ensure that students learn the great classical masterworks. Now, more and more courses are being designed to teach the history of jazz, blues, rock, and world music, as well as connections among music and the other arts, such as visual art, dance and literature. New teachers should consider areas of their own expertise and enthusiasm, whether it is opera, vocal jazz, or the music of the Beatles, and seek appropriate textbooks and outstanding recordings. Approaches to music appreciation curriculum are usually structured chronologically, beginning with early examples of a style and progressing to the present. Teachers should not feel limited by this traditional approach, and may choose to start with the music of today and work backward, or organize the course units by musical element, genre, artist, country of origin, or classification.

The College Music Society

The College Music Society (CMS) continuously examines the pedagogy and relevance of various music courses at the college level. CMS sponsors conferences that focus on provocative issues in music teaching. It has looked at the issue of teaching music history in light of the changing times and the need for new pedagogies and various repertoires, cultures and other arts. CMS is aware of the need for teachers to look beyond the history of Western art music, and supports teachers' efforts in designing courses in world music, movie music, jazz, Broadway, Tin Pan Alley, rock, rap, and other types of popular music.[8]

National Standards for Arts Education

The National Standards for Arts Education (1994) recommend the following nine music content areas that all students should know and be able to do:

1. Singing, alone and with others, a varied repertoire of music.
2. Performing on instruments, alone and with others, a varied repertoire of music.
3. Improvising melodies, variations, and accompaniments.
4. Composing and arranging music within specified guidelines.
5. Reading and notating music.
6. Listening to, analyzing, and describing music.
7. Evaluating music and music performances.
8. Understanding relationships between music, the other arts, and disciplines outside the arts.
9. Understanding music in relation to history and culture.

The National Standards apply to *all* students, including those enrolled in general music classes. Specific goals, objectives, lesson plans and suggestions for assessing the standards are outlined for grades K–4, 5–8, and 9–12 in numerous books published by MENC to assist music teachers, including *Performance Standards for Music: Strategies and Benchmarks for Assessing Progress Toward the National Standards, Grades PreK–12.*

Summary

The music education profession is made up of a diverse array of individuals who care deeply about finding ways to enrich *all* students' lives with music, no matter what their age or musical preference. Future teachers need to think beyond the boundaries of the traditional ensembles of choir, band and orchestra, which normally exclude at least 80% of secondary school students. To be more inclusive, we need to consider other possible ways to involve students in music learning activities, which might include classes in composition, guitar, or the history of jazz. Future teachers will help make our schools, our communities, and our nation more musical.

Questions, Topics and Activities for Critical Thinking

1. Observe a live or video-recorded Kodály lesson; then practice notating simple songs (such as *Joy to the World* and *Row, Row, Row Your Boat*), followed by chanting the rhythm syllables, then singing them on solfege, and finally singing while using the Curwen hand signs. For an extra challenge, practice "signing" the melody with the right hand and a simple harmonic ostinato in the left hand.

2. Observe a live or video-recorded Orff lesson; then explore words and phrases that have potential as rhythmic ostinati and phrases, such as students' names or proverbs including "An apple a day keeps the doctor away," or "A penny saved is a penny earned." Put the rhythm of the words into body percussion, and then into mallet and other percussion instruments. Create layered drones and ostinati with various words related to the phrase, and finally allow melodic improvisation using the pentatonic scale, with the rhythmic word phrase as a starting point. Can you think of any ways the Orff approach might be applied to middle school or high school music learning?

3. Observe a live or video-recorded Dalcroze lesson; then explore different musical compositions, musical concepts (pitches that move by step or skip, changing dynamics, etc.) and body movements. Discuss how you think this approach might improve musicianship for young children as well as for young adults.

4. Observe a Kodály, Orff, Dalcroze, or Gordon specialist teach an elementary general music lesson. Write a one-page paper on your impressions of the uniqueness and value of the method(s).

5. What secondary general music classes did your high school offer? Which of the secondary general music classes do you think would draw students into the music program? Which would you like to teach someday? Are there others that you would like to see included?

6. Locate *The Orff Echo* and *The Kodály Envoy* journals in your school library, read an article that interests you, and write a one-page report on an article.

7. In teams of 2–4 students, examine and identify strengths and weaknesses of current basal series textbooks used to teach elementary general music, using

criteria such as: attractiveness, durability, easy-to-follow lesson plans, extra resources, sound recording quality, yearly curriculum overview, photographic balance of genders and ethnicities, variety in styles of music, inclusion of the National Standards, cost, etc. Report to the class.

8. Register for your MENC-affiliated state organization's convention, attend several general music sessions, and discuss as a class those methods and techniques that inspired you, as well as those that you think you would do differently.

9. With your university class, take field trips to schools to observe outstanding general music teachers and write a one-page reflection of each, focusing on those teaching strategies that you found to be very effective for student learning.

10. Compile a bibliography of 15 resources on a topic of interest presented in this chapter.

Readings

Agrell, Jeffrey (2008). *Improvisation Games for Classical Musicians*. Chicago, IL: GIA Publications.

Campbell, Patricia Shehan (1998). *Songs in Their Heads: Music and Its Meaning in Children's Lives*. New York: Oxford.

Choksy, Lois (1999). *The Kodály Method I*, 3rd ed. Upper Saddle River, NJ: Prentice Hall.

Choksy, L., R.M. Abramson, A.E. Gillespie, D. Woods & F. York (2001). *Teaching Music in the Twenty-First Century*, 2nd ed. Upper Saddle River, NJ: Prentice Hall.

Demorest, Steven M. (2001). *Building Choral Excellence*. New York: Oxford.

Digest of Education Statistics of the National Center for Educational Statistics (2007) (http://nces.ed.gov/programs/digest/d07/tables/dt07_147.asp).

Findlay, Elsa (1971). *Rhythm and Movement: Application of Dalcroze Eurhythmics*. Evanston, IL: Summy-Birchard.

Goodkin, Doug (2004). *Play, Sing, & Dance: An Introduction to Orff Schulwerk*. New York: Schott.

Gordon, Edwin E. (2007). *Learning Sequences in Music: Skill, Content, and Patterns*. Chicago, IL: GIA Publications (http://www.giml.org/gordon.php).

Hickey, Maud, ed. (2003). *Why and How to Teach Music Composition*. Reston, VA: MENC.

Jaques-Dalcroze, Émile (1976). *Eurhythmics, Art and Education* (translated from the French by Frederick Rothwell). New York: Arno Press.

The Kodály Concept in America (videotape). Los Angeles: St James' School, *Episcopal*.

Lancaster, E.L. & Kenon D. Renfrow (2006). *Piano 101: Book 1*. Van Nuys, CA: Alfred Publishing.

Madura, Patrice D. (1999). *Getting Started with Vocal Improvisation*. Reston, VA: MENC.

Mark, Michael L. (1996). *Contemporary Music Education*, 3rd ed. New York: Schirmer Books.

Mead, Virginia Hoge (1994). *Dalcroze Eurhythmics in Today's Music Classroom*. New York: Schott.

Meske, Eunice Boardman (1975). "My School Has a Good Music Program–I Think!" *NASSP Bulletin, 58*(393), 5–12.

Music Educators National Conference (http://menc.org/events/view/2009-mountain-lake-colloquium) (http://menc.org/resources/view/general-music-curriculum-framework-document).

The National Standards for Arts Education (1994). Reston, VA: MENC.

Orff Schulwerk: A "Simple Gift" to Music Education (videocassette, 1997). Cleveland, OH: American Orff-Schulwerk Association.

Performance Standards for Music: Strategies and Benchmarks for Assessing Progress Toward the National Standards, Grades PreK–12 (1996). Reston, VA: MENC: The National Association for Music Education.

Saliba, Konnie K. (1991). *Accent on Orff: An Introductory Approach*. Englewood Cliffs, NJ: Prentice Hall.

Schafer, R. Murray (1988). *The Thinking Ear*. Toronto: Arcana Editions.

Schmidt, Will (2004). *World Music Drumming*. Milwaukee, WI: Music Workshops, Ltd (www.worldmusicdrumming.com).

Siebenaler, Dennis James (2006). "Factors that Predict Participation in Choral Music for High-School Students." *Research and Issue in Music Education, 4*(1), 1–9.

Silver Burdett Making Music (Grades 6, 7, & 8) (2008). Pearson Scott Foresman (www.pearson-school.com).

Steen, Arvida (1992). *Exploring Orff*. New York: Schott.

Warner, Brigitte (1991). *Orff-Schulwerk: Applications for the Classroom*. Englewood Cliffs, NJ: Prentice Hall.

Williams, David B. & Peter R. Webster (2009). *Experiencing Music Technology, Update*, 3rd ed. Boston, MA: Cengage Learning/Schirmer Books.

four
The Music Curriculum for Vocal and Instrumental Performers

FIGURE 4.1 **High school wind ensemble**

Many students entering the music education major have had a deep and satisfying involvement in their middle and high school ensembles as a choral or instrumental performer. Many have participated in several levels of their schools' choirs, bands or orchestras, as well as regular concerts, festivals, and honor groups. Few, however, have had the opportunity to learn about the details that go into creating a sequential and comprehensive music curriculum for every student. Relevant curriculum questions include:

- How many ensembles should a school have?
- How does a teacher select literature to be performed?
- What skills and knowledge should be taught in each ensemble?

This chapter will recommend ensemble curricula designed for creating comprehensive musicians.

Dr. Jenkins	Now it is time to discuss a topic that's near and dear to most of your hearts—directing music ensembles. Most of you probably attended a high school that had a strong music program, and you performed in some of the top ensembles there; and many of you have participated in your state's honor ensembles and at music camps. You were probably section leaders in your high school ensemble, and some of you even had the opportunity to assist your director in running sectionals and conducting rehearsals. On the other hand, those of you whose major instrument is piano or guitar may not have had the traditional ensemble experience, unless you accompanied the school choir, sang in choir, or played a secondary instrument.
Mario	Dr. Jenkins, I'm a violinist and I play in the orchestra here, but I had an ensemble experience that I'll bet no one else did at their school. We had a Mariachi ensemble at my high school and I really liked playing in that.
Dr. Jenkins	I'm glad you mentioned that, Mario, because it's a goal of our profession to include many different types of music in school. MENC even has a website devoted to Mariachi music (www.menc.org/gp/menc-s-mariachi-education-site). How did your director learn to play and teach Mariachi music?
Mario	I went to high school in southern California and lived close to the Mexican border, so our director brought in some local performers who worked with us and taught us how to play authentic Mariachi music and we performed with them. I played in the Mariachi ensemble for the last two years of high school, and I would really like to teach it along with orchestra when I get my first teaching job. I'm glad to hear that the music education profession encourages diverse music like that. I actually went to elementary school in Mexico, and I'd like to keep my culture alive and share it with students.
Dr. Jenkins	That's great, Mario. I hope that you'll teach this class something about Mariachi music this semester! Has anyone else performed in a diverse ensemble in school?
Amir	We had a gospel choir at my high school. My choir director let us students conduct the group because we sing gospel music in our churches, and she didn't. She let us teach the music by rote because that's the way we learn it in church. So there's no sheet music or anything, unlike all the other school choirs. I definitely want to have a gospel choir in my choral program when I'm a teacher. And I'll teach this class too, if you want to learn a gospel song.

Dr. Jenkins	We'll look forward to that, Amir, because gospel music has deep historical and emotional roots that we all should understand (Turner 2008). Anyone else?
Sung-Mei	I grew up in Taiwan, so I know some Chinese folk songs from when I was a little girl, but after I entered school the teachers only taught us Western classical music in choir and in piano lessons. We only had one choir because everyone could read music. I have so many questions about music in America. Can I have more than one choir when I teach high school? And I wish I knew more about Chinese music! Do you know if there is any Chinese music for choirs?
Dr. Jenkins	Yes, there is published Chinese choral music, Sung-Mei. As I said, the music education profession supports music of all styles and cultures, and there are publishers such as earthsongs and World Music Press that specialize in choral music from the world. You will also want to join our university International Vocal Ensemble, which performs music from all over the world. And yes, there are almost always at least two choirs in high schools in the U.S., and often several more.
Matt	I don't know if this counts as diverse music, but one thing I like to do is arrange and perform music for instruments that aren't typically used for that style. For example, I've taken a Bach Invention and scored it for vibraphone, bass and drums; and I've taken rock tunes and arranged them for classical instruments. Why do we have to play everything the same way all the time? That bores me. I'd like to teach small ensembles to arrange and perform different versions of all kinds of music.
Dr. Jenkins	So you like the *in*authentic approach! Very interesting, Matt. Here we spend so much time trying to perform music authentically, and rarely do we think about the freshness of putting it in a totally new context. That's very original thinking. Bravo!

We have discovered that while most music education majors have come from the traditional ensemble world of choir, band and orchestra, some have found their way into innovative ensembles or have other diverse interests. This is healthy for the music world and for teachers and their students. It is important to honor and preserve our traditions, yet consider new ways to include more students in the diverse musics of the world.

Ensemble Curriculum

Elementary School

Some elementary school students are fortunate to have their schools offer beginning choir, band and orchestra. It would be wonderful if all elementary schools provided not only general music instruction, but also group vocal and instrumental instruction for their students to form a strong musical foundation for future studies in the middle school and high school. MENC's *Opportunity-to-Learn Standards for Music Instruction* (1994) recommends that instruction in strings begins in the fourth grade, and in wind and percussion in the fifth grade.

FIGURE 4.2 **Fifth grade band**

Middle School

MENC's *Opportunity-to-Learn Standards* (1994) also recommends that, where enrollment justifies, there should be at least two choirs, two bands and two orchestras at the middle school level; and each should be offered at least every other day for at least 45 minutes. They should be differentiated by level of experience or age, and in the case of choirs, by voicing or gender. Other ensembles should be offered that meet the needs and interests of the school community. Beginning and intermediate instrument instruction should also be offered. The middle school might also require short six-week rotations into vocal and instrumental experiences to stimulate interest in joining the regular ensembles (Hinckley 1992). Some examples of a middle school ensemble curriculum are listed below:

Choir
    Treble Choir
    Mixed Chorus

Band
    Beginning Winds and Percussion
    Concert Band
Strings
    Beginning Strings
    Orchestra

High School

MENC's *Opportunity-to-Learn Standards* (1994) recommends that beginning, inter-mediate, and advanced choral and instrumental instruction be offered at the high school level; and that besides choir, band and orchestra, there should be at least one other ensemble for every 300 students in the school. These would include specialty ensembles such as gospel choir and jazz band. All high school ensembles should meet for a minimum of 45 minutes every other day.

FIGURE 4.3 **High school choral ensemble**

Here are possible high school ensembles:

    Choir
        Beginning Chorus
        Mixed Chorus

> Concert Choir
> Men's Glee Club
> Women's Choir
> Show Choir
> Madrigals
> Vocal Jazz Ensemble
> Gospel Choir
> International Vocal Ensemble
> Band
>   Beginning Winds and Percussion
>   Concert Band
>   Marching Band
>   Jazz Band
>   Symphonic Band
>   Mariachi Ensemble
>   Small Ensembles
>   Pep Band
> Strings
>   Orchestra I
>   Orchestra II
>   Orchestra III
>   Chamber Music
>   Fiddling Ensemble
>   Strolling Strings

Curriculum Content

Once the ensembles are organized by level of difficulty and style of music, the next important aspect of curriculum design is the sequence of skills and knowledge to be experienced within each ensemble, and also between the beginning and advanced ensemble(s). The MENC *Opportunity-to-Learn Standards* (1994) reminds us that every music course should provide development in not only the particular medium of the ensemble (e.g., developing the voice in choir, or instrumental technique in band and orchestra) but also in performing, creating, sight-reading, listening, analyzing, and evaluating a variety of types of music, as well as understanding its relationship to disciplines other than music. These should sound familiar: they are the content areas of the *National Standards for Arts Education* (1994).

Literature Selection

Some music teachers choose to use their repertoire as the basis of their curriculum. They feel that if they select high-quality music appropriate to their students' ability levels, then the concepts within the music itself become the focus. One cannot argue with the fact that a diet of masterworks is educationally and culturally important.

Philosopher Estelle Jorgensen urges music teachers to care deeply about the quality of the music they teach, and to foster knowledge and respect for great music of the Western classical tradition. She states:

> Where once it held a privileged place, it seems now to have acquired ... a negative connotation as a bastion of elitism ... Instead, popular musics ... have pride of place in much elementary and secondary music education ... designed for students whose principal fields of study lie outside of music. An all-too-common musical illiteracy or, at best, elementary level of musical literacy and aurality renders Western classical music inaccessible to the general public just as the pervasiveness of popular music renders it inaudible and invisible.
>
> (2003, 130)

Jorgensen goes on to explain the value of classical music and the danger of eliminating it from the curriculum:

> Western classical music is an intellectual achievement that appeals to the life of the mind. In its repertoire are instances of sometimes brilliant and deeply moving creations, works of exceptional talent and human genius. This music values critical and imaginative thinking ... Neglecting ... cultural treasures ... is demeaning and anti-humanistic and reveals a callous anti-intellectualist and fanaticism that runs contrary to the kinds of intellectual engagement and criticism required in humane and free societies.
>
> (2003, 136)

It is important for teachers to seek the highest quality which can be found in all kinds of music, and at the same time, to embrace many of the tenets of a comprehensive music education; namely, the activities of improvising, composing and arranging, and the inclusion of outstanding music from other cultures. Ideally, a music director will select excellent repertoire and find ways to make certain that students have the opportunity to develop their potential in varied musical skills and styles.

Skills and Knowledge

Some directors begin their curriculum preparation by focusing on the skills and knowledge to teach at each level, and then select appropriate musical compositions and arrangements. A benefit of this approach is that a sequential, comprehensive curriculum is assured; a possible drawback is that music may be selected purely for the musical skills or knowledge it can teach, regardless of whether it has artistic merit.

Selecting outstanding repertoire and designing a comprehensive approach to musicianship is a balancing act. But this is the responsibility of every ensemble director, who has a lot of freedom regarding the music curriculum and literature. This music curriculum should allow students to grow musically and artistically during the school years, and prepare them to participate in music for a lifetime. Some might continue to perform in ensembles after high school, some might major in music in college, and many others

FIGURE 4.4 **High school orchestra**

will discontinue performing but will feel a strong commitment to music and support it as an audience member.

The elementary ensemble curriculum forms the foundation for the middle school curriculum, which in turn provides the foundation for the high school ensemble curriculum. In an ideal situation, the music teachers at the elementary, middle school and high school know the importance of working together to create a sequential and comprehensive curriculum over the students' entire school years. A strong feeder program can make an enormous difference in the quality of the secondary school ensemble.

What Every Student Should Know and Be Able to Do

As stated in Chapter 3, every student, whether they participate in general music classes or performance ensembles, should achieve basic skills in the nine content areas of the National Standards for Arts Education (1994):

1. Singing, alone and with others, a varied repertoire of music.
2. Performing on instruments, alone and with others, a varied repertoire of music.
3. Improvising melodies, variations, and accompaniments.

4. Composing and arranging music within specified guidelines.
5. Reading and notating music.
6. Listening to, analyzing, and describing music.
7. Evaluating music and music performances.
8. Understanding relationships between music, the other arts, and disciplines outside the arts.
9. Understanding music in relation to history and culture.

Can you remember any examples of these standards from your high school ensemble experience?

Grading

Grading is a necessary component of teaching. It is never easy due to the challenge of finding time to accurately assess students' achievement, and because it is human nature to want to reward and encourage participation in music. So, while every teacher has to decide how to assign grades, a sample grading policy of a high-profile music performance program is provided below as a starting point for discussion and reflection.

Sample Grading Policy for a High School Band
Each ensemble member will be subjected to two playing tests throughout the course of a nine-week period and a written examination at the completion of the semester. A playing test may be given as a take home playing test and students will be responsible for turning in an audio recording with the assigned material recorded for grading purposes.

School policy for excused and unexcused absence will apply. Unexcused absences from a scheduled performance will result in a grade of "F" for the current nine-week grading period. An unexcused absence or tardiness from any *extra* rehearsals, sectionals and performances will result in the lowering of at least one letter grade for the current nine-week period.

Grading Scale for nine-week period:
    50% Playing tests
    50% Daily assessment of the following classroom expectations:
        Students will have instrument and proper supplies.
        Students will have pencil, folder and related music.
        Students will not prevent the teacher from teaching.
        Students will not prevent another student from learning.
        Students will clean up after themselves.
        Students will be prompt.
        Students will be team players.

Grading Scale for Semester:
    45% Playing tests
    45% Classroom expectations
    10% Final written exam

This sample grading plan may look familiar to many recent graduates of high school band programs. It specifies the percentages of the grade that are allocated to performance, behavior, and a written exam, and the rehearsal behavior expectations are made clear. **Would you change anything about this grading policy for the high school ensemble that you hope to conduct in the future?**

If the National Standards for Arts Education have been accepted in most states as the foundation of the music curriculum, then the assessment of students' achievement of those standards is logical and meaningful. Without assessment, it is difficult to know if or how well students have learned what was thought to be taught. Therefore, each of the nine national standards as named above has been divided into several achievement standards appropriate for elementary (K–4), middle school (5–8) and high school (9–12) music students; and specific performance standards have been developed and published to aid teachers in the strategic assessment of their students' learning. The content, achievement and performance standards are all available through MENC in hard copy as well as through its website (http://www.menc.org/resources).

The Rehearsal Structure

Every musician has been, at one time or another, a part of outstanding, moderately effective and ineffective rehearsals. What are the characteristics of a good rehearsal? **Name some characteristics of an effective rehearsal that you have recently attended.**

Rehearsal Order

One characteristic of a good rehearsal is placing faster-paced activities at both the beginning and end of a rehearsal. This engages and motivates students early in the class period, and has them depart with an up-beat piece in their musical memory. The middle portion of rehearsal may be slower-paced with the most challenging piece as its focus, or the middle portion may consist of alternating faster and slower-paced works (Cox 1989).

Pacing

Another key to a motivating rehearsal is to keep the pace quick, and not dwell on any one problem or piece for too long (Yarbrough & Price 1981). A common bit of advice for optimal attention span is to spend no more minutes than the age of the student on one activity; thus if the student is 15 years old, exceeding 15 minutes on one task may begin to tax the attention span.

The Warm-Up Period

Many teachers begin rehearsals with a five- to ten-minute warm-up to help focus the bodies and minds on the music for the day. Warm-ups are designed to teach musical skills such as proper tone, breath support, phrasing, intonation, articulation, rhythmic accuracy, and other technical or musical problems to be encountered in the rehearsal. They are often followed by sight-reading, ear-training, improvising, or theory exercises.

Artistry

Every rehearsal should achieve at least one experience of artistic beauty. While much rehearsal time is spent working on nitty-gritty details of pitches and rhythms, time must be spent on achieving the expressive potential of the music. When the students have achieved a high level of artistry for a particular chord, phrase, or balance, the teacher should take time to point it out to the students for reflection and enjoyment. Revel in those moments that inspire us all to live our life in music.

An effective 60-minute rehearsal might begin with approximately 15 minutes of warm-ups and other musical exercises such as those named in the national standards; followed by approximately 15 minutes on each of three (or more) high-quality and level-appropriate pieces. To keep interest high, those three pieces might alternate fast, slow, fast; accessible, challenging, accessible; or familiar, unfamiliar, familiar. Other possible contrasts include whole ensemble, part ensemble, whole ensemble; metric differences; and stylistic differences. These are ideas for keeping motivation and interest high during the rehearsal period (Cox 1989).

A well-executed rehearsal should resemble an interesting concert with regard to variety, with more accessible and memorable music at the beginning and end, alternating with more challenging pieces in the middle. Attention should be paid to contrasting styles, genres, keys, meters and tempos to keep student (and audience) attention high. And recognition of the unplanned and often unexpected artistic "moment," when the ensemble's musicality peaks, is of great impact. Good rehearsals are the life-blood of student musicians, and a well-organized plan will keep students active and focused on the music, which is the goal of every music teacher.

Questions, Topics and Activities for Critical Thinking

1. Did you begin your primary instrument in elementary school? If so, in what ways did you benefit from starting in elementary school rather than later?
2. If you are currently observing in an elementary music setting, what benefits do you see in starting instrumental instruction in elementary school? If your observation setting does not do this, how is it affecting the students in terms of musical achievement and interest?
3. What ensembles and general music courses did your high school offer? What does your "dream job" entail in terms of ensembles and general music courses?
4. Brainstorm as a class to compile a list of interesting ways to include each standard in a secondary school music ensemble. Discuss experiences you have had with any of these standards in your own ensembles. Did you find them valuable? Why or why not?
5. Examine the National Standards for Arts Education document to see the specific achievement goals for each of the nine content standards for grades K–4, 5–8 and 9–12. Work in small groups to create a lesson to teach one of the achievement standards for middle school or high school ensemble.
6. What kinds of things are you observing in ensemble settings that allow students to experience the activities described in the content standards? Were the activities effective?

7. In groups of four, answer the following questions regarding assessment and the sample grading policy presented in this chapter:

■ How should your grading system reflect the national standards that have been guiding your teaching?
■ Does the sample grading policy reflect national standards?
■ Do you agree that missing a performance should negate all other grades the student earned?
■ A requirement for practice is missing—do you think this is important?
■ How would this grading policy be changed for a chorus?
■ Are the expectations clear, or could you think of revisions?

8. A sample rehearsal plan format follows. At the next rehearsal you attend, see if it follows this model, and try to fill in as many of the specific parts of the plan as possible. What were the specific objectives of the rehearsal of each piece? What steps did the director take to achieve those objectives? How did the director make certain that the objectives were achieved? Was there at least one aesthetic experience of musical beauty? In class, compare and contrast this model with your observation.

Rehearsal Plan Format

Type of Ensemble:
Specific Materials Needed:
Specific Objective(s) of the Day for Each Piece:
   1.
   2.
   3.
Procedure:
   Warm-Up Activities (5–10 minutes):
      1.
      2.
      Etc.
   Sight-Reading or Other Musicianship Training:
   Piece #1 (15–20 minutes):
      Step 1:
      Step 2:
      Step 3:
   Piece #2 (15–20 minutes):
      Step 1:
      Step 2:
      Step 3:
   Piece #3 (15–20 minutes):
      Step 1:
      Step 2:
      Step 3:
   Assessment (How did the director assess if the objectives were learned?)

Readings

Band Handbook (2005–2006). Indianapolis, IN: North Central High School.

Cox, James (1989). "Rehearsal Organizational Structures Used by Successful High School Choral Directors." *Journal of Research in Music Education, 37*(3), 201–218.

Hinckley, June (February 1992). "Blocks, Wheels, and Teams: Building a Middle School Schedule." *Music Educators Journal*, 46–30

Jorgensen, Estelle R. (2003). "Western Classical Music and General Education." *Philosophy of Music Education Review, 11*(2), 130–140.

Kaschub, Michele E. (March 1998). "Standards in Action: The National Standards in the Choral Rehearsal." *Choral Journal, 38*(8), 63–72.

Keenan-Takagi, Kathleen (January 2000). "Embedding Assessment in Choral Teaching." *Music Educators Journal*, 42–46, 63.

National Standards for Arts Education (1994). Reston, VA: MENC.

Opportunity-to-Learn Standards for Music Instruction (1994). Reston, VA: MENC.

Turner, Patrice E. (December 2008). "Getting Gospel Going." *Music Educators Journal, 95*(2), 62–68.

Yarbrough, Cornelia & Harry E. Price (1981). "Prediction of Performer Attentiveness based upon Rehearsal Activity and Teacher Behavior." *Journal of Research in Music Education, 29*, 209–217.

five
The Music Educator's Communities

Tonya   I remember my high school chorus director being friendly with a lot of the other teachers in the building and even with the custodians and secretaries. He spoke to everyone and always had a positive attitude. I could tell he was genuinely happy with the school and with us. Sometimes he got special permission to take the group on tour, or to not have bus duty so he could hold extra rehearsals. In general he's a really nice guy—well liked by everyone. I'm sure that he fitted into the school very well and was respected by the other teachers and staff members.

Nick   I know there's more to being a music teacher than just teaching music. Everyone supported my high school band and everybody liked the band director. A lot of students came to concerts with their parents and usually other teachers showed up too. The director's positive attitude toward everything went a long way.

Three Communities

Teachers do not work in a vacuum. They share the joys and the challenges of their work with three communities:

- the school community
- the greater community
- the professional community (the subject of Chapter 6).

One of the keys to success in teaching music is to be a good citizen of each of the communities.

The School Community

All of the people in the school—faculty, administrators, staff, volunteers, parents and students—make up the school community, the one that music teachers interact with day to day. Every student that a music teacher works with is also a student of other teachers and is served by the school staff and volunteers. Each of these people has a vested interest in how well music students do in other classes. The wise music teacher keeps in mind that even though music is a component of a well-rounded education, the same is true of every other subject as well. All of the school personnel stand together in offering a complete education to each and every student.

One of the ways in which music teachers build a sense of community is to be interested in their students' nonmusical activities. Attendance at athletic events, art exhibits, plays, and other school events are evidence that the music educator is interested in the entire school community. Students, colleagues, and parents appreciate a music teacher who demonstrates interest beyond the classroom and rehearsal room.

The music program is demanding on students. It requires hard work and a significant amount of time and discipline for young people to be musicians. Students have crowded school and life schedules. Busy students' efforts have to be balanced with competing academic, social, athletic, and work demands. As challenging and demanding as music might be for students, their reward for a job well done is greater than the effort put into it. The teachers who meet their needs best have to be super-organized themselves to make their programs fit into school schedules and into the lives of their students. Organizing classes, ensembles, libraries, uniforms, instruments, travel, rehearsals—all of these things require efficiency, discipline, and cooperation with the rest of the school community. This is why music teachers and athletic coaches are often noted for being well organized. In small schools where there is only one music teacher, the demands can be even greater because the music teacher plans and carries out teaching strategies and programs by himself.

How does the music teacher do all of these things? There is no simple answer, except to say that the successful music teacher does them and does them well. They are done with the help, understanding and cooperation of the faculty, administration and staff.

Parents

The music teacher's strongest allies are the parents of school musicians. Parents recognize the value of music for their children and take great pride in their achievement. If a teacher inherits a music program that already has a music parent organization, it is wise to become familiar with the organization and the individuals in it. People want to help, especially when it involves their children. The parents want the music teacher to call on the organization for assistance in ways that are appropriate—raising funds, ushering, selling tickets, printing programs. That is the purpose of the organization. It is a vehicle for parents to participate in the music program while working for a worthwhile common cause.

If a teacher takes over a program with no parent organization, it is a good idea to start one. Parents will do some of the time consuming work to allow the teacher more time for specialized tasks that will help make the program stronger than it would have been without them. A busy music teacher often finds it difficult to attend evening meetings of parent organizations, but those meetings are generally very worthwhile. Not only do they offer parents the opportunity to help the music program, but they also allow parents and teachers to know each other better. As parents develop confidence in a new music teacher, they are usually more and more willing to assist in any way they can. Parent organizations are especially helpful when it comes to taking up the cause in requesting a larger music budget or any other adjustments that are needed (Elpus 2008).

Dedicated music parent organizations are not the only ones that are helpful to the music program. School-wide parent organizations like the Parent–Teacher Association (PTA) and the Parent–Teacher Organization (PTO) might offer significant help to the music program in fund raising and public relations. A good music program attracts attention, and the pride that the school and parents take in a chorus, band, or orchestra is worth a great deal to the music teacher.

Students

Teachers share the school community with their students. A sense of community allows students to develop the pride and cooperation that are needed for them to put forth their best effort. A successful choral, band, or orchestra director encourages the creation of a community within a community for the members of the ensemble so they value working together to achieve the best performance possible. Student musicians who recognize that they hold a place in a special organization are more likely to do the practicing they need to be effective members, to help others in the group, to volunteer for special responsibilities, and to be dependable and enthusiastic ensemble members. Many will also excel academically.

It is always a good idea for the teacher to promote community among students by allowing them to share in making appropriate decisions, and to assign responsibilities to willing members to serve as section leaders, assistant directors, accompanists, librarians, stage hands, wardrobe managers, and equipment managers.

The Greater Community

The greater community consists of all the individuals and organizations beyond the walls of the school. The school music program, especially the performing ensembles, should be highly visible to the greater community. The music teacher's involvement in that community includes music dealers, community music organizations, religious institutions, the board of education, and the many work and social activities that engage students outside of school. Each part of the greater community has a different interest in its school music programs.

Presenting Music to the Greater Public

The most visible musical activities that involve school musicians—concerts, parades, athletic events, and other community activities—shape the community's perception of the school music program. Public performances should please the public, but this does not mean just catering to the musical tastes of listeners. There are at least three considerations to be made in selecting music:

- Does the piece have educational value for student musicians and will it help them grow musically and technically?
- Does the piece appeal to the students?
- Does the piece appeal to the audience?

Sometimes the three criteria coincide; but at other times a piece might not suit the public's taste. As a curricular subject, however, ensembles should perform music that meets educational objectives, just as the literature that the English teacher selects should meet the objectives she sets for her class. This can create a teaching opportunity to both the students and the public. The orchestra might perform a contemporary piece that brings strange and unfamiliar sounds to the audience. It is entirely appropriate for the director to educate the audience about the piece, why it sounds as it does, how the piece benefits the students, and why it is important to perform that particular kind of music. Audiences appreciate learning about the music they hear and the orchestra will have done an important service to the school and the public by bringing a new kind of music to them. This is equally true for all of the performing ensembles at the elementary, middle school, and high school levels.

It is a good idea for a music teacher to become a familiar figure in community music, even a leader if the opportunity presents itself. The better known and more respected the school music teacher is outside of the school, the more likely that the community will support the school music program. However, the new teacher has to be careful not to take on too much, especially during the earliest stages of her career. But when the teacher has navigated the initial period, it is time to begin to look at possibilities in the greater community as a conductor, singer, or instrumentalist. Many kinds of community opportunities present themselves to music teachers.

Houses of Worship

Every community has houses of worship, and many of them hire singers and instrumentalists. If this is an area of interest to the teacher, he might find either professional or non-paid opportunities available as a singer, player, conductor, music director, leader of a children's or adult choir, or any number of other activities. While religious music offers wonderful musical opportunities, there are also disadvantages for music teachers. The teacher might not wish to give up time every weekend for religious responsibilities, and he might be required to perform at unexpected times, such as for special worship services and funerals. Like any other outside work for music teachers, it should not interfere with the school teaching responsibilities, which must always be primary in allocating work time.

FIGURE 5.1 **Private lesson**

Private Teaching

Music teachers often have opportunities for private teaching. This is a good way to earn extra income while improving teaching skills. A word of caution—it is easy to build a private teaching practice that demands too much of the teacher's time. Although a large studio is more profitable than a small one, the teacher must keep in mind that private teaching is secondary employment. Music teachers also need to be careful to avoid the appearance of profiting from their own students by accepting money for private lessons outside of school. It is better to seek private students from other schools. Music teachers sometimes cooperate with other music teachers in recommending their students to each other for private study.

Playing or Singing in Community Venues

Most communities have many cultural organizations in which music teachers participate. Community choruses, bands, orchestras, and theaters are only some of the possibilities for music teacher participation. Communities value their cultural offerings and they usually welcome the participation of music teachers.

FIGURE 5.2 **Community band rehearsal**

Music Dealers

The commercial music dealer can be one of the music educator's best friends in the community. Music teachers in communities with one or more music stores are fortunate to have a place to go to examine music, try new instruments and technology, and meet with other music educators. Although much equipment, supplies and music are purchased online now, music teachers often need to ask local music dealers for a last minute repair, for the loan of an instrument, a box of reeds or strings, or for other things that can only be provided by a local dealer. In many communities, music stores are gathering places for music teachers who feel comfortable in an inviting atmosphere that welcomes musicians and music teachers. It is a good idea to support local businesses whenever possible, especially when they are so closely related to the school music program. It is good for the program and for the economy of the community.

School and Community Together

Some music teachers have found ways to combine their school programs with adult music education. Rather than restricting a chorus, say, to young students, it might be open to adults as well. Adults love children and many want to enjoy making music with them. The combination of music and children is appealing to many adults. It also appeals

FIGURE 5.3 **Community band rehearsal**

to many youngsters who enjoy working alongside adults. The high school orchestra that is short of violists might find one among the pool of older community musicians, some of whom played viola in their high school orchestras. Adult musicians from various cultures in the community may be called upon by the music teacher to demonstrate and share their musical heritage. Teachers who do this are respected in their communities by grateful adults whose lives they enrich with music.

Older Adults

Organizations that are specifically offered to older adults are a special area of community music. Many mature adults are deeply interested in music and they want to be able

FIGURE 5.4 **Father and son perform together**

to join performing ensembles. Some played in their own student days and have not played since. Others are complete beginners who always wanted to take music lessons and play in an ensemble. Still others might have been professional musicians before they retired and wish to continue performing. Community choruses, bands, and orchestras provide a needed musical outlet for many of these people. School music teachers can also perform in these groups, and when one needs a director, the music educator is often the one best suited for that position.

An organization that caters to adult musicians is New Horizons International Music Association. New Horizons is an international network of choruses, bands, and orchestras. Members range from almost beginners to highly experienced musicians, sometimes even retired professional players and singers. For most players, however, New Horizons is the first entry point into music since their own school days. The New Horizons ensembles are so popular that there are sometimes many more applicants than they can absorb (see "Readings" opposite).

Adult music education is good for the community and good for music educators, whose students might choose to continue their music when they graduate from high school. Adults who were trained in music and now perform in the community are usually grateful for the role that music education has played in their lives and they are likely to support the school music program in any way they can.

Questions, Topics and Activities for Critical Thinking

1. Identify at least six community organizations in your community that offer some sort of musical experience, either in a performing or a classroom setting. Describe them. Tell which two you would like most to participate in and why.
2. Discuss your high school experiences as a school musician. Did you do the amount of daily practice that was expected of you? Did you have any extra responsibilities to the performing group? Did you have a sense of community in the ensemble? Describe it.
3. Did other high school teachers (not music teachers) ask you about the music program or discuss it with you? Did they come to your performances?
4. In what ways were parents involved in your school music program?

Readings

Community music. Available http://www.isme.org/en/community-music-activity/community-music-activity-cma.html.

Elpus, Kenneth (2008). "Organizing Your Parents for Effective Advocacy." *Music Educators Journal, 95*, 56–61.

Frederickson, William E. (Winter 2007). "Music Majors' Attitudes toward Private Lesson Teaching after Graduation." *Journal of Research in Music Education, 55*, 326–343.

League of American Orchestras. "Education and Community Engagement." Available http://www.americanorchestras.org/interest_areas/education_community_engagement.html.

Manfredo, Joseph (November 2006). "Effective Time Management in Ensemble Rehearsals." *Music Educators Journal, 93*, 42–46.

Miller, Rodney L. (2008). "The Impact of the American Community Band on Music Education." Available http://rave.ohiolink.edu/etdc/view?acc_num=csu1210932483; http://hdl.handle.net/2374.OX/4099.

New Horizons International Music Association. Available http://www.newhorizonsmusic.org/nhima.html.

New teacher guidelines. Available http://www.menc.org/careers/view/preparing-to-teach-music-in-today-s-schools-section-3; http://www.menc.org/documents/legislative/planning_music_ed_ad_web.pdf.

Stafford, Karen (n.d.). "Personality Conflicts." Available http://www.musiceducationmadness.com/less-than-ideal.shtml.

six
Professional Associations

The Third Community

Tonya	Dr. Jenkins, there are posters for several music education associations on the bulletin board and I'm wondering whether I should plan to join any of them now or when I begin teaching. They sound interesting, but they all charge dues and I'm not sure I can afford to join. Will they be worth the investment?
Dr. Jenkins	There are a lot of organizations for music educators that do everything from helping new teachers in their work to presenting stars of the music world at their conferences. It's up to each teacher to decide whether to join, or which ones to join. They meet practically every need that you can find in the music education profession, but you're right—they cost money, and travel to conferences can be expensive. But a lot of school districts contribute part of the travel expenses, so it's more affordable. You have to weigh all of the factors and make up your own mind.

The Third Community

Professional Associations

The previous chapter discussed two communities that music educators are a part of: school and the greater communities. There is also a third, very important, community—professional associations. Every profession has its own specialized associations that assist its members in many ways. The music education profession is especially fortunate because many associations meet both general and specialized needs of its members. All of the associations have one thing in common—they help their members grow professionally in the areas of technique, materials, and, very importantly, in developing pride in one's profession. This is called "professional development." Membership is not mandatory in any professional association, but many music teachers choose to take advantage of the numerous benefits that they offer.[1]

If membership is voluntary, then why do teachers choose to pay dues to belong to one or more professional associations? First, the professional associations—the third community—bring together teachers with like interests and responsibilities. The mutual support, education, encouragement, and camaraderie that the associations provide are vital aspects of a professional career.

Being part of a community is only one of the many benefits of belonging to a professional association. All of the associations sponsor publications. Some offer newsletters while others publish journals, teaching guides, and other print and web-based media relevant to the organization's particular interests. Some offer advocacy services. They sponsor conferences and symposia that bring music educators together to observe each other's work, listen to each other's music, examine new music and books, attend specialized sessions, and, in general, to absorb the richness of time spent with colleagues in a professional atmosphere. Some organizations sponsor research in their particular areas of interest. They publish research journals and hold sessions at their conferences where researchers share their findings.

A Sampling of Professional Associations

Associations for All Music Educators

MENC: The National Association for Music Education

MENC is the umbrella organization for the music education profession. It embraces every professional interest and involves students, teachers, the music industry, advocates, parents, and the public.

Through its many programs, activities, publications, and conferences, MENC works to ensure that every student has access to a balanced, comprehensive, high-quality program of music instruction. It promotes the best possible music education for all children. MENC advances music education through four major goals:

- Every student in our nation's schools shall study music as part of the core curriculum.
- All school music programs shall be balanced, comprehensive, and sequential, as defined in the National Standards for Music Education and shall be provided with resources as defined in the Opportunity-to-Learn Standards for Music.
- All music instruction shall be delivered by well-prepared professional music educators, each of whom meets state requirements.
- Music educators and those who support music education shall view MENC as the primary association for ensuring the widespread advancement of the profession (MENC Goals and Objectives).

The organization started in 1907, when Philip Haydn, a music supervisor in Keokuk, Iowa, issued an invitation to music educators to come to Keokuk to observe a new teaching method he had created. The invitation brought 104 educators together for three days of teaching demonstrations, concerts, publishers' displays of new music and teaching materials, and a rich exchange of professional ideas among music educators. The attendees were mostly from the Midwest, but several came from as far away as New York and Texas. The educators voted at Keokuk to found a new organization, which came into being officially in 1910, the next time they gathered together. It was named the Music Supervisors National Conference. The first meeting in Keokuk served as a model for future music education conventions, which feature the same kinds of activities and displays to this day (Mark 2008).

The term "supervisors" was selected because at that time classroom teachers taught music under the supervision of music educators. Music supervisors taught demonstration lessons and helped with lesson plans, teaching materials, music selection, and concerts. By the 1930s, the function of music supervisors had changed, and they did the actual teaching. Accordingly, the name of the organization was changed to Music Educators National Conference. The name changed again in the 1990s to MENC: The National Association for Music Education, as the number of corollary music education organizations had multiplied and the diversity of specialized teaching interests broadened. Despite its name change, the organization is still referred to as "MENC."

FIGURE 6.1 **Tonya as Collegiate MENC President**

MENC is one of the largest arts education organizations in the world, with more than 140,000 members. At any one time, the association oversees dozens of programs, initiatives, and projects. Until 2008 it sponsored national conventions every other year. Now it offers annual summer gatherings, called "academies," for its members. Its publication program is large and varied. It is the principal advocate for music education at the national level, and its officers often consult with members of Congress and representatives of the United States Department of Education. Its research activities include 14 Special Research Interest Groups, each dedicated to a particular area of music education.[2]

MENC also sponsors student chapters, referred to as CMENC (College MENC) in colleges and universities throughout the country. Although the cost of CMENC dues is significantly less than those of MENC, membership in a student MENC chapter provides all the benefits of professional membership, including access to periodicals, online journals, the MENC website, and conferences, as well as opportunities for student leaders to organize special musical and educational experiences on campus for its members. MENC recognizes outstanding collegiate chapters with annual awards. Membership in the student MENC chapter is voluntary in some universities and mandatory in others. MENC also sponsors the Tri-M Music Honor Society for high school and middle school students.

In 2009, MENC organized the Society for Jazz Education to serve the needs of its members who are jazz musicians. The Society for Jazz Education was created to replace the International Society for Jazz Education, which ceased operating in 2008.

State Associations

In addition to the national and international associations, each state has its own professional association that is affiliated with MENC. When music teachers join MENC, they automatically become members of their state associations. The state associations then receive a portion of each member's MENC dues.

International Society for Music Education

ISME differs from MENC and other organizations in a fundamental way. Although all the associations have members from outside of the United States, ISME is truly international. Its objective is to foster communication among music educators of every country of the world. Its Declaration of Belief states: "We believe that lived experiences of music, in all of their many aspects, are a vital part of the life of all people." ISME builds and maintains a worldwide community of music educators by fostering intercultural understanding and cooperation, and promoting music education for people of all ages in all places. ISME describes itself as "a worldwide service platform for music educators who want their profession to be taken seriously by educators in other disciplines, by politicians and policy makers, by international organizations that promote culture, education, conservation and durable development of cultural heritage." Its major publication is the *International Journal of Music Education*. ISME is represented in more than 70 countries through organizations called National Affiliates. MENC is the ISME National Affiliate for the United States. These are ISME's core values:

- There is a need for a worldwide community of music educators.
- There is a need for music education in all cultures.
- Effective music education depends on suitable qualified teachers who are respected and compensated properly for their work.
- All teacher education curricula should provide skills in and understandings of a selection of both local and international musics.
- Formal and informal music education programs should serve the individual needs of all learners, including those with special needs and exceptional competencies.

ISME is especially interesting for its members because its wide scope of international activities is authentically multicultural. They open a window to other cultures that would not be available otherwise. Each year the *International Journal of Music Education* features one issue focusing on important research, one on innovative practices, and one that showcases music education in countries that many American music educators know little about. The biennial conferences are held in interesting locations in different parts of the world. They give American music educators the opportunity to travel to different countries and to meet and know music educators from all over the world.

Other Music Education Associations: General Music

The American Orff-Schulwerk Association

AOSA is dedicated to the pedagogical approach of Carl Orff and Gunild Keetman. The association's mission is to:

- demonstrate and promote the value of Orff-Schulwerk;
- support professional development opportunities; and
- align applications of the Orff-Schulwerk approach with the changing needs of American society.

AOSA maintains a list of approved Orff trainers, and approved Orff I, II, and III level training courses that are offered at universities throughout the country. AOSA's major publication is *The Orff Echo*, a quarterly journal. AOSA also publishes *Reverberations*, a quarterly newsletter with lesson plans and news about members of the organization, local chapter workshops, and other items of interest. AOSA has active advocacy programs at the local, state, and national levels. In addition, it sponsors a grant and scholarship program for student assistance and research.

Organization of American Kodály Educators

The mission of OAKE is to enrich the quality of life of the people of the United States through music education by promoting the philosophy of Zoltán Kodály. OAKE has chapters on many campuses and endorses programs at about 25 colleges and universities. The organization publishes collections of music for children, bibliographies, video tapes, essays, and other teacher education materials.

More Highly Specialized Organizations of Interest to Music Educators

The following organizations are not specific to music education, although all have education components. Many school music teachers find membership in them to be valuable and rewarding.

FIGURE 6.2 **Collegiate ACDA officers**

American Choral Directors Association (www.acda.org)
American Guild of Organists (www.agohq.org)
American Music Therapy Association (www.music therapy.org/faqs.html)
American String Teachers Association (www.asta.org)
College Music Society (www.music.org)
Conductors Guild (www.conductorsguild.org)
Drum Corps International (www.dci.org)
International Clarinet Association (www.clarinet.org)
International Computer Music Association (www.computermusic.org)
International Double Reed Society (www.idrs.org)
International Horn Society (www.hornsociety.org)
International Society for Improvised Music (www.isim.edsarath.com)

International Society of Bassists (www.isbworldoffice.com)
International Suzuki Association (www.suzukiassociation.org)
International Trombone Association (www.ita-web.org)
International Trumpet Guild (www.trumpetguild.org)
International Tuba Euphonium Association (www.iteaonline.org)
Internet Cello Society (www.cello.org/index.cfm?fuseaction=Association
   Links)
Music Teachers National Association (www.mtna.org)
National Association of Teachers of Singing, Inc. (www.nats.org)
National Band Association (www.nationalbandassociation.org)
National Flute Association (www.nfaonline.org)
North American Saxophone Alliance (www.saxalliance.org)
Percussive Arts Society (www.pas.org)
VoiceCare Network (www.voicecarenetwork.org)
Women Band Directors International (www.womenbanddirectors.org)

A Broader Community of Educators

Music teachers affiliate with non-music teachers in various ways, including interdisciplinary organizations and teacher unions.

The American Educational Research Association. AERA (aera.net), an interdisciplinary organization, was founded in 1916 to improve education by encouraging scholarly inquiry in education and evaluation, and by disseminating research results. Its more than 26,000 members include teachers, administrators, researchers, graduate students, and behavioral scientists. The members are involved in education, psychology, statistics, sociology, history, economics, philosophy, anthropology, and political science. AERA sponsors numerous Special Interest Groups (SIGs), including one in music education. Its primary publication is the *American Educational Research Journal.* AERA also publishes several other journals in specialized research areas.

Teachers' Unions. The purpose of a union is to support its members in regard to working conditions and salary, to advocate for them to decision makers, and, in general, to assure that they have a high quality of life. Membership is voluntary.

The American Federation of Teachers (aft.org) is an affiliate of the American Federation of Labor and Congress of Industrial Organizations (AFL-CIO), which is an alliance of 56 national and international labor unions. Some of its members, besides teachers, are truck drivers, musicians, miners, firefighters, farm workers, bakers, bottlers, engineers, editors, pilots, public employees, doctors, nurses, painters, and laborers.

The National Education Association (nea.org). NEA advocates for educators as they prepare students to succeed in a diverse, interdependent world. Collective action through NEA allows its members to work for the common good to improve their professional status, and to provide the highest quality of public education. NEA's publication for students preparing for teaching careers is *Tomorrow's Teachers*, an annual magazine for NEA student members. It offers help with job searches and tips for the first year in the classroom. It also suggests strategies for parental and community outreach.

Questions, Topics and Activities for Critical Thinking

1. Look up MENC and ISME on their websites and explore their various projects and services. Imagine ahead to the time when you begin your first teaching job. Do you think you will be joining MENC? ISME? If yes, list several benefits that you expect to receive from your membership. If no, state why.
2. Look up the websites of the associations mentioned in your primary area of interest and list their offerings that you think will benefit you as a music teacher.
3. Find a printed program for a music education conference in your school's music library, or one that you might borrow from a faculty member. Identify the organization that sponsored the event and list the sessions you would have attended if you had been there.
4. If you have ever participated in a music education conference as a member of a performing group or as a visitor, write a one-page essay about that experience—pros and cons.

Readings

McCarthy, Marie (2004). *Toward a Global Community: The International Society for Music Education 1953–2001*. Nedlands, Australia: International Society for Music Education.

Mark, Michael L. (2008). *A Concise History of American Music Education*. Lanham, MD: Rowman & Littlefield, 90.

MENC Goals and Objectives. Available http://menc.org.

seven
What Music Teachers Need to Know to Be Successful

Elizabeth and Julian, freshman music education majors, have been discussing the different pedagogical practices they have begun to observe. These include the topics of:

- child development
- music learning theories
- urban versus rural settings
- individual differences in learning style and ability

They have also begun to discover the importance of a well-rounded education and personal integrity to their emerging roles as teachers and mentors.

FIGURE 7.1 Urban school gospel choir

Elizabeth	I had a lot of fun watching Professor Graff's demonstration of different techniques for teaching elementary general music. I especially liked how the children would hear and experience the music first, before they saw any musical notes. After all of our high school and college music theory experiences I think I've forgotten how I learned as a young child, and that's something I need to go back to and study before I get my first teaching job. It was good that Professor Graff reminded us that children learn differently than we do.
Julian	I agree. It's really important for us to recognize that children in different age groups learn differently. And what I think may be even harder for teachers is that they have to consider that within any given age group every student learns differently. I think that must be a challenge for teachers because no two brains are identical.
Elizabeth	I've been thinking about that challenge myself and especially about the differences in a large city setting versus a rural community. I grew up in a rural suburb that was kind of split between farmland and a traditional suburb, and there were mostly white middle-class kids. But ultimately I think I want to live in a city like L.A. or Washington D.C. I'm wondering what would be different about teaching in a setting like that versus where I learned as a child.
Julian	That's definitely a consideration. I grew up in Washington D.C. and I think we have to consider as teachers that not all of the learning that students do happens in the classroom. A lot of what they're learning is dependent on the environment they live in outside of class. So we need to incorporate what they're exposed to culturally inside the classroom.
Elizabeth	That's a good point. I want to learn about the culture of the city that I teach in before I start the job—just to get some background for what issues and what cultural differences I might be dealing with.
Julian	Absolutely. I think that teachers who can relate to their students are the most effective teachers.
Elizabeth	I think that overall though, whatever culture or whatever setting we teach in we have to remember that we need to be positive role models for our students. That's a lot of responsibility, especially as a young teacher, but the sense of responsibility that we will have makes me feel like I'm preparing for the most meaningful profession. It makes me really excited because I can't wait to be a teacher and be a positive influence on students' lives.

Child Development Theories

Piaget's Stage Theory

Jean Piaget (1896–1980) was a Swiss-born scholar whose influential writings about childhood cognitive development span the fields of psychology, sociology, and education (www.piaget.org). His "Stage Theory" indicates that children have distinct characteristics at each of four stages of development, and that they must pass through each stage in order to develop fundamental mental *schemas* that make the more complex intellectual processes of later stages of development possible (Piaget 1963). These schemas develop through the fitting (*accommodation*) of new information into that which is already known (or *assimilated*). The stages, their characteristics, and the approximate ages of the child are the following:

1. Sensorimotor Stage (from birth to age 2)
   - Pre-language
   - Learning through the senses, including visual, tactile, and aural means
   - Learning through motor interactions with the environment
2. Preoperational Stage (ages 2 to 7)
   - Language development
   - Symbols take on meaning
   - Learning through the senses, including visual, tactile, and aural means
   - Ability to imagine unseen objects
3. Concrete Operational Stage (ages 7 to 11)
   - Ability to perceive a cup of water as the same amount (termed *conservation*) whether it is in a coffee cup or in a tall thin vase, and is perhaps analogous to the ability to recognize the same song whether it is played on the piano or sung
   - Ability to understand musical concepts of timbre, tempo, duration, pitch, and harmony, in that order (Zimmerman 1981, 52)
   - Ability to use deductive reasoning
   - Ability to understand the world from the perspective of others
4. Formal Operational Stage (approximately ages 11 to 16)
   - Can find multiple solutions to problems
   - Can think logically
   - Can think abstractly
   - Can understand musical notation

Bruner's Theory of Child Development

Jerome Bruner (b. 1915) is an important American psychologist whose view differs from Piaget's in that the stages of child development need not be strictly sequential for advanced learning to take place. Bruner (1966) believes that the child can learn anything if she is motivated and if the environment is structured appropriately. Similar to Piaget, however, is his theory that children come to understand new information through different modes of representations, which reinforces the "sound before symbol" approaches of Kodály, Orff, and Gordon as discussed in an earlier chapter:

- Enactive—action-based (through the senses)
- Iconic—image-based (through pictures)
- Symbolic—symbol-based (through language and notation)

Vygotsky's Zone of Proximal Development (ZPD)

Lev Vygotsky (1896–1934) agreed with Piaget and Bruner that the most significant point of cognitive development in children corresponds to the use of language. He emphasized the importance of the child's social collaboration with the teacher or more advanced peers in the construction of new knowledge. The language used in these interpersonal interactions facilitates the child's learning (1978).

Suzuki's Talent Education

Shinichi Suzuki (1898–1998) begins his book *Nurtured by Love* (1983) with the observation that all children can speak the language of the culture into which they are born, no matter how difficult we might consider that language to be (such as the various Japanese dialects). Suzuki concluded that children are capable of learning anything, as Bruner theorized, if presented in the correct manner. He called this the "mother-tongue method" (p. 3), which corresponds to the sound (the language of the mother's voice) before symbol (written language) philosophy of teaching children. He emphasized that talent is not inherited, but nurtured. As soon as children are born it is essential to provide a rich home environment of beautiful music to develop the ear. He also stated that with daily focused practice on an instrument, every child can develop high-level musical ability within ten years (see www.suzukiassociation.org).

Milestones of Musical Development

Although children learn at different rates, a general guide for understanding and thus developing the basic musical capabilities of children is as follows (Gordon, http://www.suzukiassociation.org; Shuter-Dyson & Gabriel 1981; Zimmerman 1981):

- Birth to ages 2–4: Absorbs and unconsciously collects sounds of the music in the environment; moves and babbles in response to these sounds.
- Ages 2–4 to ages 3–5: Imitates with some precision simple tonal and rhythm patterns of music in the environment; can hear differences in pitch registers (high/low).
- Ages 3–5 to ages 4–6: Can hear differences in dynamic levels (louder/softer); can perform simple rhythmic and tonal patterns; can coordinate singing, breathing and moving.
- Ages 6–7: Can hear differences in tempos (faster/slower) and vocal intonation begins to stabilize.
- Ages 7–8: Can hear differences in timbres, as well as consonant and dissonant sounds.
- Ages 8–9: Rhythmic performance begins to stabilize.
- Ages 9–10: Can hear and perform simple harmonies, and melodic performance begins to stabilize.
- Ages 10–11: Harmonic ability begins to stabilize.

General Learning Theories

No matter whether a learner is a child, an adolescent, or an adult, there are some general principles of learning and teaching that can be applied to all ages.

Motor Skill Development

Motor skills are needed for all music making. In fact, Frank Wilson (1987) calls musicians "small muscle athletes." The development of motor skills progresses through these three stages:

1. A basic approximation of the skill.
2. Increasingly refined motions.
3. Smooth execution without any mental concentration on the motions.

The corresponding role of the teacher in the progression of the developing motor skill is as follows:

1. Intensive teacher instruction.
2. Decreasing amounts of teacher feedback.
3. Independence from the teacher (Uszler, et al. 1991).

Any teacher can think back to a recently developed motor skill (e.g., a difficult musical passage or a new sport) and recall the early stages of the mental focus and guidance required before it started to feel natural.

Cognitive Development

Cognition refers to mental activities such as remembering, thinking, creating, and problem solving. A taxonomy of cognitive goals in education was developed and published by Benjamin Bloom (1956). Six major goals for learning are the following:

1. Knowledge
2. Comprehension
3. Application
4. Analysis
5. Synthesis
6. Evaluation

It is easy to understand why these goals are arranged in hierarchical order by recalling that learners may reach goal #1, *knowledge*, in order to pass a test by knowing the correct answers to questions, even when they do not fully *comprehend* (goal #2) the meaning of the information. And just as students may *comprehend* the information, they may not be able to *apply* the principles of that information to a new setting (goal #3), or *analyze* it into its smaller parts (goal #4), etc. Therefore, the Taxonomy of Educational Objectives can be a helpful guide for teachers in developing various levels of thinking skills in their students.

Affective Development

The affective realm of music education refers to one's preferences, tastes, and values in music. Music educators expect to influence their students' taste and values, and they can learn strategies to do that. Some studies have found the following results:

- Musical taste can be influenced by several sources, including aspects of the music such as its complexity, meaning and performance quality, but also by family, peer groups, media, musical training, personality, gender, and maturity (LeBlanc 1980).
- Increased familiarity with a musical selection breeds preference for it up to a critical point, at which time repeated hearings of the selection breed increased dislike of that music. This is called an inverted-U function (Hargreaves 1986).
- Likewise, increased complexity breeds preference for a musical selection up to a point, at which time repeated hearings breed increased dislike of the music due to an overload of information (Hargreaves 1986).

Diverse Learning Styles

Students, young and old, learn in different ways—some find visual aids to be especially helpful in understanding a concept, some prefer to listen to aural examples or verbal instructions, and still others learn best if they can be physically involved. In order to accommodate all students' learning styles, teachers need to provide instruction that utilizes all three modes of learning—visual, aural, and kinesthetic—whenever possible (Conway & Hodgman 2009). Visual learning might occur through reading materials, posters, video-recordings, PowerPoint presentations, or teaching demonstrations; aural learning might occur through the teacher's verbal explanations, class discussions, recorded musical examples, or teacher modeling of a desired tone; and kinesthetic learning might occur through movement-based games, dances, instrument fingerings or expressive exercises.

Besides preferences for the perceptual modalities of aural, visual and kinesthetic learning, students also have cognitive and affective style differences. Some of the cognitive (thinking) style dichotomies are listed below, and students may fall on one end or the other, or somewhere in between (Gumm 2003):

- Detail-oriented versus Holistic-oriented
- Active versus Reflective Learner
- Concrete versus Abstract Thinker
- Prefers Closed versus Open-ended Solutions
- Distracted versus Focused
- Rigid versus Flexible
- Close-minded versus Open-minded

Affective (feeling) preferences may fall along the following continua:

- Class Participant versus Non-participant
- Competitive versus Collaborative

- Social versus Aloof
- Preference for taking information in versus for constructing their own meaning
- Preference for Structured Goals versus Unstructured Goals

These learning preferences show us that our students may learn in very different ways from which we learned, and that we, as future teachers, must try to accommodate all learning styles by expanding our own teaching styles beyond what feels most natural for us.

Culturally Diverse Learner Behavior

Students of different cultures often have very different expectations for classroom behavior. Without an understanding of different cultures' norms, the music teacher may misunderstand a student's behavior and inadvertently stifle learning. An obvious example of such a misunderstanding is the student with Limited English Proficiency (LEP) who fears and avoids speaking aloud in class. The teacher may consider the student to be quiet, or shy, or unintelligent, while all three of these characteristics may be far from the truth. Teachers must be aware and knowledgeable of possible cultural differences of students in the music classroom.

In the book, *Approaches to Behavior and Classroom Management* (2009), Scarlett, Ponte, and Singh explain some fundamental differences among cultures. In some cultures, for example, children might be trusted to manage their own behavior because they know that their responsibility is to the harmonious group, and the teacher rarely intercedes. In other cultures, however, the teacher assumes an authoritarian approach to emphasize strict discipline, order, and control; a frequent consequence of breaking a rule is public shame. Consider the confusion of a child who is of a different culture than most or all of her classmates and is unfamiliar with the cultural norms that guide the classmates.

The authors also explain that many different cultures are often represented in American classrooms. One culture might emphasize group dynamics over individual contributions, so students may need more guidance with regard to the teacher's expectations for individual work. In another culture where respect for elders and cooperation in groups are the norm, small student-led discussion groups may be the most effective way to involve the student in learning. Yet other cultures may encourage individuality and independence, and the teacher may then need to encourage collaborative activities among peers. Teachers obviously need to be sensitive to the cultural differences in student behavior and find ways to bring out the best in each student (Scarlett, et al. 2009).

Urban Music Education

Teaching in an urban school can be enormously rewarding and meaningful despite the characteristic challenges of teaching many students from poverty-stricken homes (and some homeless), leaving them disadvantaged in terms of educational opportunities and hope for the future. Students are often considered "at-risk" for failing to succeed in school and in life for reasons ranging from teenage pregnancy, alcohol or drug abuse to the AIDS virus and lead poisoning. But parents, teachers and administrators who care deeply about the success of these students can make a positive difference. While individualized instruction, high expectations, a strong attendance policy, early intervention, and parental involvement are all important to keeping at-risk students in school, we know that they must be motivated to stay in school. There is plenty of evidence that the arts can be particularly motivating and helpful to at-risk students (Taylor, et al. 1997).

FIGURE 7.2 **First grade violin student**

Inspiration and concrete ideas for dynamic music programs for at-risk students can be found in two volumes of a book published by MENC, titled *Teaching Music in the Urban Classroom* (2006). Many of these programs are based on partnerships between arts organizations or university music programs and public schools. For example, one partnership is providing violin lessons for all 46 first graders in one disadvantaged school in Bloomington, Indiana; similarly, a social worker from the Minneapolis Public Schools was moved by one homeless seven-year-old who loves to play the violin and commented that music serves as a balance for homeless children, and that "students are more resilient if they are able to develop musical skills" (Kingbury 2009, 42–43). Another partnership provided an after-school music program for first through fifth graders in inner-city Los Angeles, which resulted in increasing enrollments each week and unforgettably rich and fulfilling musical experiences for both the children and the student teachers (Ward-Steinman 2006).

One new music teacher found that in order to engage his Phoenix inner-city students he needed to move his mindset "from Haydn to hip-hop," despite having no interest in it previously. He commented:

> In order to best meet the needs of my students, I had to step outside of my realm of experience and challenge myself to be and take part in something new. I believe that this willingness to change and grow is key for any music educator who wishes to be successful in a culture that is different than his or her own.
>
> (Vagi, in press)

Gender

Gender also plays a part in classroom dynamics and learning. Developmental levels are slightly different between the genders with girls developing verbally more quickly than boys. Music teachers need to be sure to encourage a balance of classroom participation between girls and boys, and that gender equality is evident in course content, whether that includes musical role models, instrument choice, or potential careers in music (Curzan & Damour 2006).

Special Education

Every student, including those with cognitive, sensory, neurological, physical and other health disabilities, deserves music instruction and opportunities. The law (*Individuals with Disabilities Education Act*—IDEA) requires that instruction be *inclusive* in the least restrictive environment (LRE), as well as adapted to meet the individual needs of these students. About half of the students eligible for special education services have specific learning disabilities, followed by speech and language impairments (19%), mental retardation (11%), emotional disturbance (8%), other health impairments (5%), autism (1.4%), orthopedic impairments (1.3%), hearing impairments (1.2%), and other disabilities.

It is not possible to list all of the strategies known to be effective for special education students in the music classroom because the specific learning disabilities of 50% of these cases include a range of problems including visual-spatial motor processing, problem solving, language, and social skills, which may or may not effect learning in the music classroom. Close work with school staff will be needed to identify and create the student's Individualized Education Program (IEP). Outstanding resources for specific accommodations in the music classroom are *Music in Special Education* (Adamek & Darrow 2005) and *An Attitude and Approach for Teaching Music to Special Learners* (Sobol 2008).

In general, for the majority of these diverse-ability students, it is helpful for the music teacher to provide:

- highly structured activities
- simple, explicit instructions
- clearly defined expectations

- large visual aids
- obvious aural aids
- modeling and imitation
- multimodal presentations
- plenty of repetition and practice
- plenty of time for processing and responding
- patience and positive reinforcement
- peer tutoring
- excellent music.

Certainly the music educator will need to understand the characteristics of each of the disabilities, and this information will be available in future teacher certification coursework, and from the school's counselors and other support staff (Atterbury 1990; Welsbacher & Bernstorf 2002; Adamek & Darrow 2005; Sobol 2008).

Gifted Education

There is no single accepted definition of the gifted student, although the National Association for Gifted Children (NAGC) offers this: "Students who give evidence of high achievement capability in areas such as intellectual, creative, artistic, or leadership capacity, and who need services and activities not ordinarily provided by the school in order to fully develop those capabilities" (www.nagc.org).

Some students have exceptionally greater musical abilities than their peers. The music teacher's role is to help gifted students and their parents recognize their special abilities and provide them with encouragement and knowledge so they can develop their musical potential to the fullest. The teacher can also help in the following ways:

- By assisting the student in setting high goals for achievement.
- By providing opportunities for the students to demonstrate their talent.
- By being a mentor, or locating a mentor, who can model and nurture "advanced levels of expertise and creativity" in musical potential (Pleiss & Feldhusen 1995; Feldhusen 1996).

Music Education Research

With regard to the development and diverse learning theories and practices presented in this chapter, it should be noted that new research is being conducted and published continually. Therefore, none of the theories stated are to be regarded as absolute truth, but rather the current state of knowledge which is bound to expand. By reading professional journals and books, attending conferences, and pursuing advanced degrees, an educator can stay abreast of new research findings in music learning and effective teaching throughout one's career.

Professional Ethics and Personal Integrity

Teaching is a profession that requires ethical behavior and integrity. Music teachers influence students in many ways beyond course content, and often serve as role models for their students. Therefore, professional conduct and ethics, as well as personal integrity, are essential for the safe and just education of students in the impressionable years of public schooling.

Code of Ethics

A code of ethics is a set of principles regarding the core values of a profession. It is developed to guide practice and professional judgment (http://www.highered.nysed.gov/tcert/pdf/codeofethics.pdf). Teachers' codes of ethics vary from state to state. Due to increasing public awareness of teacher violations of ethical behavior, including sex scandals involving teachers, some school districts require teachers to attend courses in proper teacher conduct (Jonsson 2001). Breaches of ethics also include teachers altering student standardized tests for bonus pay, drug and alcohol infractions involving their students, and avoidance of "whistle-blowing" on fellow teachers known to be engaging in unethical behaviors (Colnerud 1994).

Some codes of ethics are stated in positive terms, such as the New York State Code of Ethics for Educators (http://www.highered.nysed.gov/tcert/pdf/codeofethics.pdf) which lists six major principles, followed by clear explanations and expectations for each. The principles are:

1. Educators nurture the intellectual, physical, emotional, social, and civic potential of each student.
2. Educators create, support, and maintain challenging learning environments for all.
3. Educators commit to their own learning in order to develop their practice.
4. Educators collaborate with colleagues and other professionals in the interest of student learning.
5. Educators collaborate with parents and community, building trust and respecting confidentiality.
6. Educators advance the intellectual and ethical foundation of the learning community.

Other codes of ethics are framed in terms of violations of professional conduct, with detailed examples of each, such as the Iowa Code of Professional Conduct and Ethics (http://www.boee.iowa.gov). Some violations of ethics that music educators should be aware of are named below:

1. Crimes, sexual or other immoral conduct with or toward a student.
2. Misrepresentation, falsification of information.
3. Misuse of public funds and property.
4. Violations of contractual obligations.

5. Unethical practice toward other members of the profession, parents, students, and the community.
6. Incompetence.

New music teachers need to be aware of the professional conduct expected of them and should read carefully the code of ethics for the school district in which they become employed. Consequences of inappropriate teacher behavior can result in the loss of teacher certification for life.

The Teacher/Student Relationship

While all teachers want to be liked by their students, the mature teacher knows that there must be a professional distance between them. Despite the close emotional bond that teachers and students feel in the music-making experience, teachers should guard against being alone in a room with a student, touching a student, or making verbal or emailed comments that could be misinterpreted as mutual affection. In this day and age of law suits, the teacher must be aware of potential problems and avoid situations with opportunities for inappropriate interactions (including electronic interactions) with students. Students have been known to make false accusations against teachers for improper behavior, not to mention real accusations that have cost music teachers their teaching certification.

Personal Integrity

Personal integrity is related to professionally ethical behavior, but pertains to one's *character*. *The Stanford Encyclopedia of Philosophy* refers to integrity as the complex quality of a person's character, which is "uncorrupted," whole, persistent, adaptable, and communicative. People with integrity "stand up for their best judgment within a community of people trying to discover what in life is worth doing ... and have a sure grasp of their real moral obligations" (Cox, et al. 2008, 1–19). Perhaps the simplest and clearest definition of integrity is "doing the right thing when nobody's watching" (Dean Bandavanis, as cited in Wald 2009, A26).

The following descriptors come to mind when one reflects upon the integrity of music teachers:

- Fair
- Honest
- Trustworthy
- Concern for others
- Humble
- Encouraging
- Respectful
- Strong in principle when under pressure
- Consistent in action and words

Integrity is a vital character trait that future teachers should value as they prepare to be positive influences, role models and mentors for the thousands of young musicians they will encounter during their careers. Teaching is a noble profession that requires music educators' best efforts. Music experiences that we provide can uplift the spirits of all of our students, improve the quality of their lives, and help them to become more ethical, just and caring human beings (Woodford 2008).

Copyright Law

Another aspect of ethical teacher behavior is respect for and compliance with the U.S. Copyright Law. Many music educators see little harm in photocopying music because they have witnessed it done so often. While few teachers are ever fined or sued for abusing the copyright law, it can and does happen. It is the responsibility of the teacher to respect the rights of the composer/arranger and publisher, and to teach students to do so as well. Ignorance or a small music budget is no excuse to break the law. Here are a few relevant aspects of the law:

- The copyright law *does* permit copying music in the emergency of an imminent concert date, but it also requires that the same music be purchased regardless of whether it is needed after the performance;
- the law prohibits purchasing music but then making copies to preserve the original scores;
- the law does not permit photocopying more than 10% of a complete work, even for educational purposes;
- out-of-print music may not be photocopied without explicit permission granted by the publisher of the work; and
- compositions or arrangements with an expired copyright or that never had a copyright are considered "public domain" and are free to copy.

Penalties for infringement of the copyright law can range from $750 to $250,000 in fines and/or imprisonment. The complete copyright law and its implications are available online at www.copyright.gov, and copyright issues specific to music can be found through the Music Publishers' Association of the United States at http://mpa.org/copyright_resource_center/copying (Ward-Steinman 2010). Copyright law specific to music can be found on MENC's website (http://www.menc.org/resources/view/united-states-copyright-law-a-guide-for-music-educators).

Questions, Topics and Activities for Critical Thinking

1. Draw a comparison chart of the child development theories of Piaget, Bruner, and Suzuki, and reflect on the importance of knowing these theories to your future as a music teacher.
2. Refer back to the topic of Elementary General Music in Chapter 3, and discuss which aspects of the Kodály and Orff approaches fall into Piaget's and/or Bruner's stages of development. Then, in small groups or individually, create a

mini-lesson plan for a child between the ages of six and seven, based on your new knowledge of how children develop.

3. Discuss how an understanding of the development of the motor, cognitive and affective abilities will make you a better music teacher. Write a two-page paper on how a specific personal experience (as a musician or as a teacher) supports each of the three theories of learning.

4. In teams of two, prepare a mini-lesson that emphasizes at least two of the three modes of learning—visual, aural, and kinesthetic—and have the students in your class identify which modes you used. As a class, discuss the effectiveness of each mode. Additionally, make a note regarding which mode(s) you preferred in each lesson and notice trends to determine your own and others' preferred modes of learning.

5. From the list of cognitive and affective dichotomies identified above, identify those that seem to match your own preferences. Share these with the class. Notice if there is a wide range of learning preferences in your class, or if music education majors tend to have the same preferences. Notice the dominant learning and teaching styles in your other music classes and non-music classes.

6. Reflect on one student you knew in high school or earlier who had a disability or was "at-risk" and write a one- to two-page paper on how a music class made a positive difference in the student's life.

7. Reflect on a class in which you felt misunderstood or like an outsider in terms of learning styles or cultural differences. How did you feel, and what was done or could have been done to help you feel more comfortable? Last, decide how you can use this experience in your own teaching.

8. Refer back to the Code of Ethics for New York and Iowa teachers, and discuss how each of the points can be applied to music teaching. Then find the Teachers' Code of Ethics for your state, read it thoroughly and discuss it in class.

9. Write a three- to five-page paper on the importance of teacher ethics and integrity, citing your sources.

Readings

Adamek, Mary S. & Alice-Ann Darrow (2005). *Music in Special Education*. Silver Spring, MD: The American Music Therapy Association, Inc.

Atterbury, Betty W. (1990). *Mainstreaming Exceptional Learners in Music*. Englewood Cliffs, NJ: Prentice Hall.

Bloom, Benjamin S., ed. (1956). *Taxonomy of Educational Objectives: The Classification of Educational Goals; Handbook I: Cognitive Domain*. New York: David McKay Company, Inc.

Bruner, J. (1966). *Toward a Theory of Instruction*. Cambridge, MA: Belknap Press of Harvard University Press.

Colnerud, Gunnel (1994). Loyalty conflicts in teacher ethics. RIEJUL1996 ED392738.

Conway, Colleen M. & Thomas M. Hodgman (2009). *Teaching Music in Higher Education*. New York: Oxford University Press.

Cox, Damian, Marguerite La Caze & Michael Levine (2008). "Integrity." In *Stanford Encyclopedia of Philosophy* (http://plato.stanford.edu/entries/integrity/, retrieved 2/20/09).

Curzan, Anne & Lisa Damour (2006). *First Day to Final Grade*, 2nd ed. Ann Arbor, MI: University of Michigan Press.

Feldhusen, J.G. (1996). "How to Identify and Develop Special Talents." *Educational Leadership,* *53*(5), 66–69.

Frierson-Campbell, Carol, ed. (2006). *Teaching Music in the Urban Classroom, Volumes I and II.* Lanham, MC: Rowman & Littlefield Education.

Gumm, Alan (2003). *Music Teaching Style: Moving Beyond Tradition.* Galesville, MD: Meredith Music Publications.

Hargreaves, David J. (1986). *The Developmental Psychology of Music.* Cambridge: Cambridge University Press.

Heath, S.B. (1978, 1983), as cited in Scarlett, Ponte & Singh (2009), *Approaches to Behavior and Classroom Management: Integrating Discipline and Care.* Thousand Oaks, CA: Sage.

Jonsson, Patrik (2001). "When Teachers' Ethics Come into Question." *Christian Science Monitor* (http://www.csmonitor.com/2001/1106/p11s1-lekt.html, retrieved 2/21/09).

Kingsbury, Kathleen (2009). "Keeping Homeless Kids in School." *Time, 173*(11), 42–43.

LeBlanc, A. (1980). "Outline of a Proposed Model of Sources of Variation in Musical Taste." *Bulletin of the Council of Research in Music Education, 61,* 29–34.

Madura Ward-Steinman, Patrice (2006). "Learning to Teach Music in the City: Privileged Music Education Majors Reach Underprivileged Children in an After-School Music Partnership." In Frierson-Campbell (ed.), *Teaching Music in the Urban Classroom: A Guide to Leadership, Teacher Education, and Reform,* Vol. II (pp. 115–122). Lanham, MD: Rowman & Littlefield Education.

Madura Ward-Steinman, Patrice (2010). *Becoming a Choral Music Teacher: A Field Experience Workbook.* New York: Routledge.

Piaget, J. (1936, 1963). *The Origins of Intelligence in Children.* New York: W.W. Norton & Company, Inc.

Pleiss, M.K. & J.F. Feldhusen (1995). "Mentors, Role Models, and Heroes in the Lives of Gifted Children." *Educational Psychologist, 30*(3), 159–169.

Scarlett, W. George, Iris Chin Ponte & Jay P. Singh (2009). *Approaches to Behavior and Classroom Management: Integrating Discipline and Care.* Thousand Oaks, CA: Sage Publications.

Shuter-Dyson, R. & C. Gabriel (1981). *The Psychology of Musical Ability,* 2nd ed. London: Methuen.

Sobol, Elise S. (2008). *An Attitude and Approach for Teaching Music to Special Learners.* Lanham, MD: Rowman & Littlefield and MENC.

Suzuki, Shinichi (1983). *Nurtured by Love: The Classic Approach to Talent Education,* 2nd ed. Smithtown, NY: Exposition Press.

Taylor, Jack A., Nancy H. Barry & Kimberly C. Walls (1997). *Music and Students at Risk: Creative Solutions for a National Dilemma.* Reston, VA: MENC.

Teaching Music in the Urban Classroom (2006). Reston, VA: MENC.

Uszler, Marienne, Stewart Gordon & Elyse Mach (1991). *The Well-Tempered Keyboard Teacher.* New York: Schirmer Books.

Vagi, Robert (in press). "From Haydn to Hip-Hop." *Teaching Music.*

Vygotsky, L.S. (1978). *Mind and Society.* Cambridge, MA: Harvard University Press.

Wald, Matthew L. (2009, May 13). "Hearing Suggests Inattention by Pilots Before Buffalo Crash." *The New York Times,* pp. A1, A26.

Welsbacher, Betty T. & Elaine D. Bernstorf (2002). "Musical Thinking Among Diverse Students." In Eunice Boardman (ed.), *Dimensions of Musical Learning and Teaching* (pp. 155–167). Reston, VA: MENC.

Wilson, Frank R. (1987). *Tone Deaf & All Thumbs?* New York: Vintage Books.

Woodford, Paul G. (2008). Democracy and Music Education. In Michael L. Mark (ed.), *Music Education Source Readings from Ancient Greece to Today,* 3rd ed. (pp. 352–353). New York: Routledge.

Zimmerman, M.P. (1981). "Child Development and Music Education." In *Documentary Report of the Ann Arbor Symposium.* Reston, VA: MENC, pp. 49–55.

eight
Competencies That Music Teachers Need to Be Successful

FIGURE 8.1 **Nick conducting a middle school band**

Experience, Experience, Experience

There is no substitute for experience when it comes to successful teaching. Every little bit helps, whether it is working as a summer camp counselor, assisting at a high school during a break from college classes, directing a church choir or musical theater production, or teaching in an after-school music program. Through these experiences, the novice teacher learns first-hand how to relate to students and also how to apply the teaching techniques discussed in music education classes. One learns the importance of organization, patience, repetition, and encouragement. One observes that students learn differently; some respond best when there is a visual aid, while another learns best when the teacher models the desired technique. The shy novice teacher will learn that when she "acts" confident, the students will be more attentive; and the jokester will find that when she learns to balance her serious and humorous demeanors, her students will be well behaved and eager to please. The confidence and skill gained through taking advantage of teaching experiences is invaluable.

College students will have plenty of opportunities to refine their teaching skills through practice-teaching their peers in your music education courses. In addition, they will be required to spend numerous hours "in the field," observing, assisting, and practice-teaching in public school music classrooms and rehearsals. The usual sequence of these formal field experiences that accompany many music education courses begins with structured observations in various well-run K–12 music classrooms. These observations start as early as the freshman year in college.

In addition to field observations, another type of field experience is one that involves assisting a school music teacher. Later, usually in combination with general, choral and/or instrumental methods courses taken during the junior year, students teach in school classrooms, at first conducting warm-ups or teaching simple songs, and later rehearsing music or teaching full lessons. These experiences lead comfortably to the actual student teaching experience, where upper-classmen spend a full semester of their senior year in residence in a public school, assuming many responsibilities of the full-time music teacher. The university's student teaching coordinator partners with a seasoned mentor music teacher to place the student teacher in the most appropriate setting for her growth. The student teacher is observed and evaluated numerous times during the semester. She sometimes decides to reside near the public school and experiences the first semester away from the college. It is a time of tremendous personal and professional growth, complete with the joys and frustrations of teaching students who are not yet yours, but under the supervision of your master teacher.

Throughout all of these field experiences, music education majors learn to think deeply about effective teaching through the use of structured observation, reflective journaling, and class seminars. They learn to self-evaluate their developing teaching skills through the frequent use of video cameras and supervisor evaluations. The video camera is an extraordinary learning tool because students can see exactly how they appear to others. It is natural to focus on the negative aspects of one's teaching at first viewing, but it is important to note both strengths and weaknesses when self-evaluating, and provide suggestions for improvement for the next opportunity to teach. This combination of field experiences coupled with a variety of modes of self-evaluation of teaching is an excellent way to put the theory of the university music classroom into effective practice.

Lesson Planning

Every lesson needs a plan. The teacher should have a specific objective in mind for what the students will learn and how they will demonstrate their learning during and at the end of the lesson. There needs to be a well-thought-out approach to breaking down the lesson into small steps, leading from what the students already know to the unknown. The lesson's steps should be designed to involve the students in multiple modes of learning:

- visual
- aural
- kinesthetic

In addition, the teacher should plan to use effective strategies such as:

- teacher modeling of the desired skill, and
- student practice (repetition or drill) of the skill.

The teacher should also find multiple ways to assess whether the students are really learning the task, such as through:

- individual demonstration,
- small group demonstration, and/or
- question and answer.

The following format for a lesson plan requires ten pieces of information.

1. The class and age level for which the lesson is planned.
2. The objective of the day's lesson (name the skill or musical concept to be learned).
3. The learning outcome, or the way in which the student will demonstrate achievement of the objective.
4. A list of specific materials needed for the lesson.
5. An indicator of specific previous knowledge (or what the students already know that is a necessary prerequisite to the current lesson).
6. An attention-getting opening to the lesson (this can be anything from an interesting question asked by the teacher to an outstanding recording).
7. A numbered step-by-step sequence of activities that takes the learner from the previous to the new knowledge or skill by changing one thread at a time. An example is the change from "hate" to "love" by changing one letter in each step.

   Hate
   Rate
   Rote
   Rove
   Love

8. Assessment strategy. This step states how the teacher will check student progress during (formative assessment) and at the conclusion (summative assessment) of the lesson. It is important to remember to assess small groups or individuals to make sure that at least 75% of the students have learned the lesson. Sometimes the class leaders will give the impression that all the students are learning, but without checking a representative sample, the teacher will not know for sure.
9. Feedback to the student. It is important to give specific feedback to the students

each time they respond to the teacher's instruction, so that they can understand and monitor their own learning.

10. Follow-Up. Here the teacher will note what was accomplished as planned and what revision or repetition is needed before moving on to the next lesson. It is best to do this right after the lesson while the experience is fresh.

The objective of a lesson is often termed a "behavioral objective" which specifies how the learners will demonstrate in some active way their achievement of the objective (a new skill or musical concept), and thus provide the teacher with a means for assessment. Action verbs are used to express the means by which students will demonstrate their learning—they might "*walk* to the beat," or "*place* objects in order to demonstrate the form of the piece," or "*play* the scale" or "*sing* the correct rhythm," or "*write* an essay" (Hackett & Lindeman 2010).

The behavioral objective requires four pieces of information to guide the lesson:

- Who learns? ("*The first grade general music student ...*)
- What musical concept? (*... will demonstrate an understanding of steady beat ...*)
- What action verb? (*... by walking to the beat ...*)
- What conditions? (*... while singing 'Teddy Bear, Teddy Bear.'*")

Some actions are easily observed while others are more difficult; for example, it is impossible to hear whether *every* chorus member can *sing* the passage just rehearsed. Because it is the teacher's responsibility to assess everyone's learning, she may ask individual rows to sing the passage, or "everyone with a birthday in June." This will aid the teacher in knowing whether most of the individuals are achieving the objectives, or if only the "ringers" or strong singers are carrying the group. If the teacher moves on before the majority of the students have learned the material, she is doing a disservice to her students.

In review, assessment is key to every lesson, both during (formative assessment) and at the conclusion (summative assessment) of the lesson. It is important to follow assessment with specific teacher feedback to the student. This is referred to as the *complete teaching cycle*:

1. The teacher gives instructions.
2. The students respond.
3. The teacher provides specific feedback (Yarbrough & Price 1981; Price 1983).

Assessment should also be used to provide feedback to the students' parents, and especially to the teacher about the effectiveness of her own teaching. If student progress is lacking, she can repeat the lesson with new strategies and/or additional practice. Assessment benefits everyone involved in the learning process and is guaranteed to improve instruction.

Complete your lesson plan now to fit into the lesson plan format below, and submit it to your professor at your next class meeting. Be sure to keep a copy for yourself so that you can begin to memorize the plan.

> <u>*Music Lesson Plan*</u>
>
> *Date:*
> *Type of Class and Grade Level:*
> *Behavioral Objective:*
> "The <u>university freshman</u> student … (who learns?)
> … will demonstrate understanding of <u>two-against-three rhythm</u> … (what concept?)
> … by <u>tapping</u> two subdivisions of the beat in their left hand, followed by three even subdivisions in their right hand, and finally both together … (what action verb?)
> … <u>while the teacher models on a snare drum</u>" (what conditions?)
> *Specific Materials Needed:*
> *Specific Previous Knowledge:*
> *Attention-Getting Opening Statement or Activity:*
> *Procedure (include timing in minutes per step):*
> *Step 1:*
> *Step 2:*
> *Step 3:*
> *Step 4:*
> *Etc.:*
> *Assessment:*
> *Formative:*
> *Summative:*
> *Feedback:*
> *Follow-Up Ideas for Next Lesson:*

Now that you have written a good lesson plan, the next step to effective teaching is the actual presentation of the lesson. How does a teacher make a lesson effective and interesting? Are there certain strategies that teachers use to enliven their lessons? Is there a certain personality that makes a better teacher?

Personality

There is not one personality type that succeeds in teaching; the successful teacher is one who finds the right fit with her musical skills and preferences and with the students' age level. Some teachers prefer to nurture the musical seeds in small children; others desire a competitive marching band scene. A large urban school system or international teaching opportunities attract some future teachers, while the small rural school where the music educator teaches all grades interests others. While teachers come in a variety of personality types, some ranging from energetic to relaxed, from imaginative to practical, and from casual to formal, it is not the personality that determines someone's success as a teacher (Gumm 2003). When we think of our favorite teachers, it usually comes down to those who genuinely cared about their students and about the quality of their learning experiences. In fact, most students remember the teachers that cared the most over those who knew the most.

On the other hand, there are teaching *styles* that are associated with effective teaching that the novice teacher can develop (Gumm 2003). Most new music education majors have thought little about the importance of eye contact, body language, speech speed and volume, positive reinforcement, quick pacing, and learning every student's name quickly. Future teachers can and should develop these and other important skills regardless of whether one has an introverted or extroverted personality, or a serious or humorous nature. It may be especially vital for those who have been primarily solo musicians, such as pianists and guitarists, to attend to these characteristics as they prepare to teach large ensembles in the schools.

Eye Contact

Scenario: Steve is a student teacher in a California middle school and is conducting the chorus while being observed by his music education professor from the university. The professor sets up a video camera in the back of the room to avoid being a distraction to the students. She turns the camera on and Steve begins his lesson. Steve is a fine singer and musician, and is an intelligent and friendly young man. However, what his professor notices immediately is that Steve's head is buried in the musical score, and he is rarely looking up at his singers. Because the choir's sound is quite good, Steve doesn't notice what his professor notices: that every girl in the back row of the chorus is involved in something other than singing! One is putting on make-up, another is doing homework for another class, two are texting back and forth, and one is napping! If Steve had looked up, he would have noticed, but because he was depending only on his ears, he assumed everyone was singing because the choir had leaders with strong voices. The professor thought it would be an interesting lesson to videotape the activities of the girls in the back row so Steve could observe what was really happening in his rehearsal.

This true story is only one example of what can occur without the teacher's eye contact.

What harm was caused by Steve's lack of eye contact with the students? How could he have rectified this situation before the end of class? What should Steve do to prepare for his next rehearsal?

Teacher Magnitude

There are several teacher characteristics that have been found to improve "magnitude," or the dynamic presence of the music teacher, which in turn improves student attentiveness. These include the ways teachers can vary their body movement, gestures, facial expressions, vocal volume and inflection, and pacing (Yarbrough 1975; Yarbrough & Madsen 1998; Madsen 2003).

Movement, Gesture, and Facial Expressions

The effective teacher does not stand in one place in the classroom, but rather walks close to students to keep their attention. The effective teacher uses a variety of facial expressions and gestures. These characteristics may need to be practiced by the less naturally dramatic music education majors. There is a certain amount of acting in teaching, and these skills can be easily achieved with practice.

Speech

Consider the aspects of a teacher's voice that can be varied: its volume, range, speed and inflection. When the teacher uses an expressive, rather than monotone voice, sometimes speaks loudly and other times very softly, and can vary speech speed, the class is bound to be more attentive. Sameness breeds inattention.

Positive Reinforcement

Also related to variety in speech is the use of reinforcement or feedback. It is important to balance both encouraging feedback with specific suggestions for improvement. Positive reinforcement does improve student attitudes, but students will begin to "tune out" praise if it is constant and nonspecific. An example of balanced feedback would be, "Excellent posture, but take a bigger breath this time so that you can sing through the whole phrase."

Pacing

A quick pace in the music rehearsal is conducive to attentiveness and on-task behavior. It is important to keep all talking to a minimum and music making to a maximum; and to provide frequent activity changes. This takes preparation, energy and enthusiasm on the part of the teacher (Yarbrough 1975; Yarbrough & Madsen 1998).

Modeling

Verbal versus nonverbal teaching also exemplifies variety in use of speech. Modeling is as effective as explaining how to sing a certain vowel, or achieve a particular tone. Students are often impressed, interested, and motivated when their teacher demonstrates fine musicianship for them, so this strategy should be widely used. If describing is necessary, it is wise to keep one's words to a minimum so that their impact can resound in the memory. Too many words can cause students to tune out while short phrases of seven words or less, such as "Let's repeat, with dynamics this time, please!" are a direct and effective approach to speaking in a rehearsal (Archibeque 1992).

Scenario

Phil, a student teacher, is directing a middle school band while his university professor is observing the rehearsal. Phil is an intelligent but quiet individual. He finds it difficult to think of the right words to say when he stops the band from playing. He tries to analyze the problem after his cut-off, but takes too much time before speaking to the group, leading to classroom discipline problems and general disorder. Phil's supervising teacher at the middle school gives him a failing midterm grade because of his inability to teach in a more spontaneous and enthusiastic manner. Phil's professor suggests that he go somewhere where he can practice shouting enthusiastic praises, such as "Excellent tone, Clarinets!" or "Outstanding sight-reading, Students!" or "Let's try that again, at Letter A!" Phil thought this was a humorous approach to his problem and gave it the good old college try. Not only was he able to begin using these in his rehearsals, but his supervising teacher gave him a grade of A in student teaching and stated that he had never seen a student teacher improve so much in such a short amount of time.

The moral of this true story is that with practice of effective teaching techniques, even a student with a shy personality (albeit intelligent and motivated) can develop the characteristics needed. Phil went on to be a successful high school orchestra director in a high-profile public school district.

Summary

The music teacher must be aware of those characteristics that he can manipulate to keep students' interest: eye contact, body language and facial expressions, speech speed and volume, modeling, feedback and positive reinforcement, quick pacing, and complete teaching cycles. While it may not be natural to one's personality to use these dramatic effects, they have been shown to improve student attitude and attentiveness, which are prerequisites to learning and achievement. Therefore, every teacher should practice these techniques. Every teacher is a little bit of an actor.

Musicianship and Performance Skills

A music teacher must be a solid musician, a competent performer of a primary instrument, a skilled conductor, and a decent pianist. She must be able to sight-read, hear errors, analyze, and know the historical importance of musical scores. She must be able to arrange a musical score to fit the limited instruments or voices in his ensemble.

None of the musical skills identified above is unimportant, even if they may seem so to a freshman or sophomore in college. They are all needed to succeed as a music teacher, as reported by first-year teachers when asked for advice from current music education majors. The student teaching semester or the first year of teaching is too intense a learning experience to try to catch up on piano skills for warming up the choir, or developing independence of hands in conducting. Weak areas need to have been mastered during the previous four years of study. The music education major should be known as the university student who can do it all, not the one "who can't play, so teaches."

Music education majors are expected to do more than other music majors. In addition to the music core of music theory and aural skills, music history, ensembles and private lessons that all music majors take, the music education major also has a full slate of techniques and methods courses in general, choral and instrumental music; as well as courses required by law for teacher certification, usually offered by the university's

FIGURE 8.2 **Practice, practice, practice**

School of Education. It is natural for music education majors to have few opportunities to take elective courses because of the heavy coursework. They usually take very full course loads each semester to complete the degree and certification requirements within four to five years. These heavy course demands, coupled with the diligent study required to achieve a strong grade point average (GPA) for teacher certification, and practice to prepare the public recital required of the music degree, often seem more than humanly attainable. So, the path to music teacher certification is far from easy. But the world has always needed and will always need music and music teachers, and the prospects for employment and a satisfying professional life for those who desire this path are very good.

Familiarity with Teaching Materials: Textbooks and Repertory

Courses in vocal and instrumental techniques and methods will provide undergraduates with a comprehensive supply of fine resources for their teaching career. Techniques courses in brass, woodwinds, strings, percussion and voice are usually offered early in the music education major's plan of study. These are followed by choral, general, and instrumental methods courses which are offered later in the degree program so that the ability to play, repair, and teach the various instruments is fresh in the mind of the student teacher. These courses are designed to enable the student to teach a variety of music courses to all ages of students. Studies in music repertory for school ensembles are also provided, sometimes as a unit within a methods course, or as a separate literature course.

Preparation in a Secondary Teaching Area and/or Level

Most music education majors enter college with a fairly clear idea of what level of music student they would like to teach after graduation. If they work very hard, they will find themselves well prepared to teach every level, and are open to most possibilities for employment. New graduates may find their dream job right out of college, but most are willing to accept the best position they can find during the summer following graduation. Some with dreams of teaching high school band find themselves teaching elementary school band and loving it; others hoped to teach high school choir and find themselves accepting a job as a middle school general and choral music teacher. It may take a few years before the ideal position in the ideal location is advertised and offered, so music education majors must be prepared for that event by studying and practicing those subjects that may not be their primary areas of expertise. Sometimes a secondary area becomes a primary area as a result. Flexibility predicts better marketability.

Leadership Skills

A leader is a person "in charge" and who inspires others to follow. We have all known leaders in our lives—in school, in clubs, in church, and with friends. Some people seem to be natural leaders and others are more comfortable as followers. Yet, clearly a teacher must be a leader if she is to be in charge of not only her rehearsal, but of a music program. She will be called upon to bring her school music groups to community events, to promote her music programs, and to speak on behalf of music education. How does one develop the leadership skills that these expectations require? What inspires a leader?

In fact, anyone with passion, knowledge and skill can be a leader in their particular field of expertise. When skill, knowledge and passion come together, leadership skills can be developed. Colleges and universities provide students with those skills and knowledge, but the spirit and passion comes from within. It is important for students to "find their bliss," whether it is teaching strings to young children, directing a high school choir, teaching middle school band, or general music. They must work hard to develop the expertise, and then believe in their abilities and engage others with their enthusiasm. Enthusiasm is contagious, and others will follow their inspiring leader.

A few suggestions for developing strong leadership skills are provided by MENC (http://www.menc.org/v/higher_education_admin/what-makes-a-good-leader and http://www.menc.org/v/higher_education_admin/17-tips-for-effective-leadership-in-any-field):

- See things from the perspective of the people you are leading.
- Have compassion for others.
- Delegate tasks to others who can handle them.
- Thank your hardworking volunteers with small gifts and public recognition.
- Cultivate your sense of humor.
- Stick to things until you finish them.
- Show enthusiasm.

- Have high expectations of people.
- Be trustworthy and trusting.
- Communicate regularly.
- Be a good listener.
- Be patient.
- Accept blame for problems.
- Be fair to all.
- Love what you do.

And finally, Warren Bennis (1997, 163) inspires us with one paramount trait of good leaders: **Good leaders must have a strong sense of purpose and be willing to take action and learn from their mistakes.**

Questions, Topics and Activities for Critical Thinking

Questions

1. What experiences have you already had that you think will help you be a good teacher? How will you continue to gain the experience needed to be an effective first-year teacher?
2. Brainstorm about scenarios that use the "Complete Teaching Cycle." Have you observed teaching situations where the teacher's instructions were left out of the cycle? Or the students' response? Or the teacher's specific feedback?
3. Discuss the effective teaching techniques described in this chapter. Can you think of others? Also discuss any distracting mannerisms or habits that college students may want to avoid when teaching, such as ending every instruction with an "OK?" or referring to the students constantly as "you guys."
4. Think of leaders that you have known and discuss as a class the characteristics of these leaders. Do they all have similar qualities, or do they come in a wide variety? What specific things have they done to inspire you to participate in ways that you otherwise would not have?

Activities

1. Think of a skill or topic for a short (ten-minute) lesson that you would like to teach your peers. Consider a subject in which you are already an expert and about which you are enthusiastic. Then draft a step-by-step lesson plan following the ten steps listed in the chapter. At the next class, discuss the aspects of designing the lesson that were the most challenging.
2. Finally write a lesson plan using the format provided in this chapter, and practice it in front of a mirror or video camera while exploring teacher magnitude techniques. Prepare to teach it to your peers in class.
3. Teach a ten-minute music lesson to your class following the guidelines of this chapter, and while being video-recorded. After viewing the video, self-evaluate your teaching, and write a one- to two-page report identifying five of your teaching

strengths as well as five areas you would like to improve in future teaching experiences.

4. Invite a guest conductor to your class to present basic conducting gestures, including beat patterns, various preparatory beats, and independence of hands.

5. Prepare one short approved piano piece, patriotic hymn, or set of scales as part of this course's requirements.

6. Prepare one short performance piece on your primary instrument for an in-class recital.

7. Identify one composition used in your high school that you found effective. Required information includes title, composer or arranger, type and level of performance ensemble, and reasons for the piece's effectiveness (e.g., what did it teach you?). The professor will compile the list for all.

8. Observe music classes in public schools and the university, and for the first two classes complete the Structured Observation Form below. At later observations, focus specifically on other topics of this chapter suggested by your professor, which may include the following questions:

- What was the objective(s) of the lesson?
    - What approaches to teaching the objectives were used? (Visual? Aural? Kinesthetic? Modeling? Question and Answer? Repetition and Drill? etc.)
    - Which of these modes seemed to be the most effective for student learning?
    - How much time was spent on each activity?
- How were the students assessed regarding their achievement of the objective?
    - Was there formative assessment? Summative assessment?
    - What kinds of feedback were given? Was it specific? Encouraging? Honest?
- Approximately how much teacher talk versus student talk versus music making occurred?
- How much teacher "magnitude" was observed? What aspects of the teaching were varied for dramatic effect—Voice volume? Speech speed? Inflection? Gestures or other body movement? Eye contact?
- Did the teacher demonstrate his or her own musicianship? How? Was it effective? Why?

Structured Observation Form

Date of Observation: Grade Level Observed:
Class Observed:
Describe the appearance of the room. Is it orderly? Interesting? Welcoming? Distracting?

Describe how the teacher gets the students' attention and begins the lesson.

Describe what students are expected to learn during this day's lesson.

What techniques did the teacher use to make sure the students learned the lesson? Visual aids? Aural aids? Modeling? Explanation? Repetition? Questioning? Physical Movement?

Describe the students' attentiveness, participation, and attitude during the lesson.

How did the teacher end the class?

What did you find effective about the lesson? What would you do differently?

Readings

Archibeque, Charlene (September 1992). "Making Rehearsal Time Count." *Choral Journal*, 18–19.

Bennis, Warren (1997). *Managing People is Like Herding Cats*. Provo, UT: Executive Excellence Publishing.

Gumm, Alan (2003). *Music Teaching Style: Moving Beyond Tradition*. Galesville, MD: Meredith Music Publications.

Hackett, Patricia & Carolynn Lindeman (2010). *The Musical Classroom: Backgrounds, Models, and Skills for Elementary Teaching, 8/E*. Upper Saddle River, NJ: Prentice Hall.

Madsen, Katia (Spring 2003). "The Effect of Accuracy of Instruction, Teacher Delivery, and Student Attentiveness on Musicians' Evaluation of Teacher Effectiveness." *Journal of Research in Music Education, 51*(1), 38–50.

Price, Harry E. (1983). "The Effect of Conductor Academic Task Presentation, Conductor Reinforcement, and Ensemble Practice on Performers' Musical Achievement, Attentiveness, and Attitude." *Journal of Research in Music Education, 31*(4), 245–257.

Yarbrough, Cornelia (Summer 1975). "Effect of Magnitude of Conductor Behavior on Students in Selected Mixed Choruses." *Journal of Research in Music Education, 23*(2), 134–146.

Yarbrough, Cornelia & Katia Madsen (1998). "The Evaluation of Teaching in Choral Rehearsals." *Journal of Research in Music Education, 46*(4), 469–481.

Yarbrough, Cornelia & Harry E. Price (1981). "Prediction of Performer Attentiveness based upon Rehearsal Activity and Teacher Behavior." *Journal of Research in Music Education, 29*, 209–217.

nine
Challenges for the New Teacher

Alongside the supreme joys of a career making and teaching music are the struggles that new teachers experience, which often include learning how to manage the music budget and other administrative duties, student discipline issues, and balancing career and home life. Other challenges may include learning to adapt classes to students with special needs, to communicate with parents, to fund-raise, to advocate for the music program, and to arrange music for the available instrumentation or voices (Vartanian 2003). It is important that the student begins to think about the realities of and solutions to inevitable challenges.

The first couple of years of teaching are the most challenging because not even the best music education department, nor outstanding field experiences, can fully prepare the student for his first real classroom of students. There are matters that are idiosyncratic to each school that have to be learned on the job, including such aspects as the history of the music program prior to the new teacher's arrival, the nature of music programs in the feeder schools, school policy on behavior and safety, community relations, the school's demographics (e.g., ethnicity, socioeconomics, and location), not to mention the personalities of the staff, students, and parents. Fortunately many schools now assign a mentor teacher to new teachers to help them navigate the challenges of the new position. In the meantime, however, an awareness of the problems and possible solutions common to new teachers can help prepare the music education major for the challenges of the profession.

Classroom Management

One of the biggest challenges for new teachers is managing behavior, particularly disruptive behavior, in the classroom. Music teachers, however, are fortunate in that the majority of their students elect to participate in music class, and so discipline issues are relatively rare. An effective approach to classroom management is for the teacher to exhibit positive behavior by beginning class on time, and keeping the students active,

FIGURE 9.1 **A well-focused high school choir**

the pace quick, and the content challenging. Learning all of the students' names quickly and using good eye contact are other effective behavior management techniques. And while the emotions of adolescents often run high, the teacher should refrain from taking their negative comments personally. Many tense situations can be resolved with a positive, caring, and humorous manner (Madura Ward-Steinman 2009).

The teacher can avoid many behavior problems by clearly communicating class rules, procedures, and consequences to students from the first day of class. The behavior of the students during the first week will be indicative of their behavior throughout the school year. For example, students need to know the *procedures* of what to do in the following situations:

- when the bell rings to start class
- when another person is speaking
- when to be absolutely quiet and when talking is allowed
- when they are dismissed at the end of class
- if they are late to class
- if their instrument needs repair
- if they have a question
- if they feel sick
- if they need to use the restroom

- if a visitor enters the classroom
- if there is a fire drill, and more.

While procedures illustrate the manner in which the rehearsal will run smoothly, there must also be *rules* that clarify unacceptable behaviors. Five unacceptable behaviors are:

- Aggressiveness
- Dishonesty
- Defiance
- Disruptiveness
- Uncooperativeness (Collins 1999).

Music class procedures, rules and consequences may be printed in a course handbook given to all students, written into a contract signed by the students and parents, or may be posted in the rehearsal room. The *consequences* should be carefully planned, and might include the following, depending upon the number of offenses and/or the seriousness of the infraction:

1. Warning.
2. Name written on the board.
3. Penalty such as demerits toward the class grade.
4. Detention.
5. One-on-one talk with the student outside of class.
6. Phone call to the student's parents (the teacher should assume a non-threatening tone in order to find support from the parents).
7. Send the student to the principal's office.

Students have the right to learn in a classroom free from disruption; and it is the teacher's responsibility to assure that the learning environment is positive and functional. The teacher who enforces the rules and consequences consistently and fairly sets the stage for productivity and can enjoy a well-managed music program.

Even with a carefully executed management plan, however, some students act out for reasons that are beyond the teacher's control. At the early signs of this, it is to the teacher's advantage to speak with the school counselor to learn if there is a history of family, medical, or psychological problems with the student. The counselor assists teachers in implementing effective strategies for working with these individuals (Madura Ward-Steinman 2010).

Business Matters

Preparing a Music Budget

Many new teachers struggle with managing the music program budget. The amount of money in the music budget as well as the procedures for making purchases can vary widely from district to district. Normally, there are separate budgets for categories such as supplies, equipment, music, and maintenance, and either the music teacher or the music department chairperson must complete a purchase order for each item needed. For some large items that exceed the allocated budget, the merchants must submit formal bids. The bidder who offers the best quality at an acceptable price will be selected. For maintenance items, such as piano tuning, a regular schedule and separate budget may be established by the school district (Hansen 2002).

The new teacher will need to carefully plan and keep records of purchases so as not to exceed the budget for which he is responsible. These procedures need not be overwhelming as long as an administrative secretary or a mentor teacher provides support and information for budgeting. The support may come through assistance with the first music order, in sharing expertise in writing a grant proposal, and/or in contacting an established fundraising company (Vartanian 2003).

If the music budget is generous, money may be available for not only sheet music, supplies and repairs, but also for large items such as a new sound system or platform risers. However, if the music budget is minimal, the teacher may need to use materials that the school already owns or borrow from other schools. In fact, rarely is a music budget adequate for the many expenditures of large ensemble programs and their associated travel expenses. Fundraising has become a necessity for most performing groups, with one survey indicating that 91% of school music programs participate in fundraising activities. Students often sell candy, pizzas, trash bags, or hold car washes to help fund special music events.

Fundraising is often facilitated by a booster club made up of dedicated parents of the music students. Booster clubs generally establish by-laws, policies, and procedures for money collection procedures, and teachers are advised to avoid handling moneys raised by the booster club. Those funds should be kept in a separate account, and expenditures should be approved by the club's officers (Hansen 2002). Parent volunteers are often willing to set up the booster club as a nonprofit entity whose tax status exempts it from paying taxes because there are no shareholders who earn profits from the value of shares. This status, usually 501(c)3 of the tax code, is granted by the United States Internal Revenue Service.

Parents are a vital part of the success of a large program, and contribute greatly to the impact of the program on the community, and overall public relations (Wiehe 2008). For the new teacher with little experience with such an organization, a mentor teacher is often available to assist with the social and organizational skill needed to succeed. If no music mentor teacher is available, MENC provides mentoring through its website at www.menc.org. An organizational resource is MENC's *Music Booster Manual* (1998).

Some parent/teacher organizations offer scholarships or grants to school music programs that have special needs. A music teacher who learns how to write an effective grant proposal is often the beneficiary of these funds (Hansen 2002). Some tips for preparing grant proposals include the following:

- Communicate with likely financial supporters (arts patrons, business partners, alumni, parents, etc.) in person, by phone, and through mail.
- Ask to see successful grant proposals from previous years to use as a model for writing your own.

- Articulate in writing the need for and purpose of the funds.
- Articulate how the students and others will benefit from the funds.
- Prepare a detailed budget and timeline for the request.
- Articulate how the funds will be used and who will supervise their use.
- Proof-read all written work for spelling and grammar errors, and communicate in a professional and gracious manner.

Planning Tours

Students love ensemble tours, and many join ensembles because of these trips. In the first few years of teaching, however, it is advisable to plan short tours so that all of the organizational logistics that go into a longer trip can be learned over time to ensure success in future excursions. Even a short tour will reveal to the new teacher a number of essential organizational matters, such as the following:

- Begin planning well in advance of the tour, even a year or more.
- Know the school's procedure for ordering transportation for the ensemble's tour.
- Require parent permission slips, contact information and medical release forms for all students.
- Organize more than enough chaperones in the event of illness or emergency.
- Provide chaperones with emergency teacher contact information and clear expectations for their responsibilities on the tour.
- Provide all students and chaperones with a clear date, time, and place for departure on the tour.
- Strict rules of conduct and dress code must be enforced, even when not performing.
- Close supervision (unannounced visits, curfew) of students in hotel rooms is critically important.
- For longer tours, use a professional booking agency and get recommendations from other trusted directors (Phillips 2004).

Teacher Portfolios

The Interstate New Teacher Assessment and Support Consortium (INTASC) was created in 1987 to guide the states in the reform of the preparation, licensing, and continued professional development of new teachers. It developed model core standards for teachers, as well as licensing examinations and performance assessment in the form of a portfolio. As a result, most new teachers are required to develop a portfolio as part of the certification process. The portfolio is usually in a three-ring binder that shows authentic evidence of knowledge, performance and disposition regarding the core standards.

The five major principles that provide the foundation for the standards are these:

- Teachers are committed to students and their learning.
- Teachers know the subjects they teach and how to teach those subjects to diverse learners.

- Teachers are responsible for managing and monitoring student learning.
- Teachers think systematically about their practice and learn from experience.
- Teachers are members of learning communities (INTASC 1992).

The core principles were later revised for the fine arts for the purpose of licensing teachers of music, visual arts, theater and dance (INTASC 2002). These documents have guided the states in the creation of their licensing standards for teachers, and most undergraduate students spend much time preparing their professional portfolios with documentation of teaching competence, and continue to refine their portfolios as new teachers (www.ccsso.org/projects/interstate_new_teacher_assessment_and_support_consortium). The portfolio may include the following:

- Teaching materials.
- Samples of student work.
- Video-recordings of teaching and student learning.
- Audio-recordings of the teacher's musical performance ability.
- Teacher assessment records.
- Teacher concert programs and reviews.
- Teacher reflections on teaching and learning issues.

In the early stages of the development of the professional portfolio, music education students may ask themselves several questions (Johnson, et al. 2006):

- What do I want to place in my portfolio to show my strengths as a music teacher?
- How can I best organize my evidence for effective presentation?
- Is my portfolio cover professional looking and is my table of contents clear?
- Do my narrative introductions to each piece of evidence clearly relate to the particular teacher standard?
- How much evidence is enough and how much is too much?
- Does my evidence really show my unique personality and talents?
- Are my video-recordings of teaching exemplary of my best work?
- Are my audio-recordings exemplary of my best musical performances?
- Do my reflective writings show depth of thought about teaching and learning issues?
- Can I improve my portfolio by removing earlier work when I add new evidence?
- Have I proof-read the entire portfolio thoroughly?

Numerous resources for portfolio development can be found in this chapter's references.

The new teacher should continue to develop the professional portfolio for future job interviews, and revise it accordingly as teaching experience and expertise accumulate. Improved documentation should replace earlier items, and evidence of teaching and musical achievements as well as student growth should be presented. It is good practice to continue to collect verification of all important activities, and to update and re-organize the comprehensive collection yearly. The teacher may prepare different port-folios for different job interviews (elementary versus secondary teaching, or general music versus conducting) and for application to graduate school. The portfolio may be rearranged depending on specific purposes and to keep it from becoming unwieldy in size.

Another solution to the unmanageable increase in size and weight of the portfolio after years of collecting artifacts of one's teaching is to create or transform an existing portfolio into an electronic one. Some students are intimidated by the technological knowledge needed to create an e-portfolio but it is to their benefit to become acquainted with the technology.

Technology

It is virtually impossible to keep completely current with changes in technology. But there is no doubt that music technology is here to stay and that it is an effective tool for enhancing teaching and musical experiences. The electronic portfolio is an excellent example of how technology provides the opportunity to store the artifacts that fill up numerous heavy binders onto a CD-ROM that can be easily edited, transported, mailed, and provided to multiple employers while still keeping the original.

PowerPoint and Microsoft Word are often used in e-portfolio construction because they are easily and widely used by university students and teachers. Other software products that vary in ease of use include music notation programs like Sibelius and Finale, and FileMaker Pro, Portfolio Assessment Toolkit, Movie Player Pro, Hyper-Studio, Macromedia Authorware, iMovie, Claris Home Page, Adobe Acrobat Exchange, Microsoft Office Works, FrontPage, AppleWorks, and iWork (Wyatt & Looper 2004). The hardware needed, which includes computers, printers, scanners, digital cameras, and CD-ROM drives, is readily available in most universities. Specific "Dos and don'ts for developing an e-portfolio" (p. 43) as well as multiple resources can be found in Kersten's (2004) article "E-Portfolio for the Internet Job Hunt."

Seven categories of music technology, as identified by Williams and Webster (2008), are the following:

- Computer and Internet Concepts
- Capturing, Editing, and Storing Digital Audio
- Multiple Tracks and Channels of Digital Audio
- MIDI Sequencing and Digital Audio
- Sound Shaping and Synthesis
- Music Notation
- Computer-Aided Instruction

Music teachers will find that knowledge and skill in these areas of music technology are very beneficial for themselves (as well as their students) in projects such as recording and burning CDs for school ensembles, designing music for plays, and arranging and printing professional-looking musical scores. Students can benefit from computer-aided instruction (CAI) in practicing sight-reading, ear-training, listening, improvising and composing skills; and they will enjoy learning how to add sound files to their personal websites. The book *Experiencing Music Technology* (Williams & Webster 2008) provides the teacher with software and hardware specifications, ideas on projects that address the National Standards for Arts Education, and accessible approaches to understanding the multiple ways technology can support music teaching.

Personal Time Management

Musicianship

Many new teachers are so busy with all of the requirements of the new job that it is difficult to find time for their own needs, particularly continuing their own musical growth. They often find that their performance skills suffer due to lack of time to practice or study, yet it is the quality of teachers' musicianship that inspires their students to also achieve greater levels. There are plenty of opportunities to continue to perform, including community bands, orchestras or choirs; church choir or accompanying jobs; free-lance "gigging" for weddings, parties, pit orchestras or nightclubs; or regular meetings (or "jam sessions") with other adult musicians to play in small ensembles in their homes. It is important to seek out opportunities to make music in order to keep performance skills strong and to provide the joy that only music making can bring.

Keeping one's performance area strong is just one of the priorities that the new teacher needs to identify and protect. It is one's professional and personal growth that provides a good role model for students. Again, a music mentor teacher can assist the new teacher with a time-management plan that organizes his priorities. The plan may include the identification of one's most important goals to achieve a balance among school responsibilities, musical enrichment, healthy lifestyle, family commitments, and recreation. While this balance is not easy to achieve, it is essential to a happy, healthy, and productive life.

Advanced Degrees

Some states require that teachers complete their master's degrees within a certain length of time after beginning to teach, while other states have no such requirement. Nevertheless, after a period of time teaching in the schools, it is natural to want to refresh the mind and achieve higher levels of musical and academic stature through graduate school. Some teachers choose to study areas of music education that were unavailable to them during their undergraduate studies, and return to focused study on their instrument or conducting. Some graduate programs are available during the summers or during a one-year leave of absence from the teaching position, so that the teacher does not need to leave a teaching position. Some students choose to take a break from public school teaching and pursue graduate study full time for two years, and then return to teaching or pursue doctoral work that will allow them to prepare future music teachers and conduct research at the university level. There are many ways for music teachers to stay musically and academically strong throughout their professional careers.

Advocacy

Advocacy is simply telling one's story to decision makers, such as parents, school administrators, members of local and state boards of education, state legislatures, and

FIGURE 9.2 **Graduate student explaining his research project**

high-level federal government officials like the Secretary of the United States Department of Education and members of Congress. All of these people control decisions that ultimately affect music education at the local level, in individual schools. Basically, advocacy consists of helping people understand why music education is important enough to deserve the support it needs to be successful. There are some basic things that advocates for music education need to know to be effective. They need to know who makes decisions about music in schools, whom to advocate to, what to advocate for, and the role of decision makers in supporting school music programs.

Every board of education has to make difficult decisions about the most effective way to spend the funds that are allocated to it. Sometimes there is enough money to fully support all of the school programs. Other times, though, there is not enough money and some programs have to be reduced. Maybe the board decides not to fill vacant positions of retiring teachers. Or to hire only new teachers because their salaries are lower than those of experienced teachers. Or to reduce the music budget for the music program for purchasing uniforms and instruments. Even worse, instrumental music might be eliminated for, say, fourth graders, or an entire music program might be eliminated. Fortunately, although these things have happened, most programs have found ways to survive and flourish, and their success is often due to effective advocacy efforts.

FIGURE 9.3 **Advocacy in action: Taya Avery addresses the Johnston, NC Board of Education**

Every music teacher is an advocate for music education, even those who are new to the profession. Although new teachers seldom have the opportunity to speak to their boards of education, they often speak at meetings of parent organizations. So how will the beginning music teacher fit into the advocacy picture? He will be an effective advocate by building the most successful music program possible. When parents, teachers and other community members see their children succeeding in music, they know how important music education is. Parents appreciate their children's musical growth and take pride in it. They will be friends of the music program when they see their children growing musically and they will make their pride known to the administration. If this sounds like a music teacher just carrying on from day to day, always doing his best work, that is exactly what it is.

Later in his career, when he has more experience working with parents and administrators, he might have the opportunity to address the board of education about the valuable work students and teachers are doing in the music department. When possible, it is a good idea to present a brief program of live music to demonstrate how successful the student musicians are, both technically and musically. This is one of the most persuasive ways to make decision makers supporters of the music program. It gives board members the information and inspiration to make them friends of the program who will support it when they have to make difficult decisions about allocating a limited amount of money.

One of the basic problems of advocacy is that it is difficult to persuade decision makers of the value of music education because they themselves may not have experienced the life-changing power of music. Music teachers are musicians who know deep in their being how music affects people. They want their students to share the benefits and joys of music education that have enriched their own lives. The challenge is that it is difficult to express in words how music affects people. Music has to be experienced. No matter how heartfelt a verbal presentation might be, board members who have not actually participated in music might not hear an explanation in the same way that the presenter feels about it. This does not mean that advocates should not use words to promote their cause. It just means that advocates have to be very well prepared to present their case and to take advantage of every opportunity to demonstrate the value of music education.

Why Advocacy Is Needed

Why is advocacy needed for a subject that has proven its value in every known civilization for thousands of years? Why, especially if the principal, the other teachers, the superintendent and the parents support music enthusiastically and there is no financial difficulty? The answer is that teachers of every subject are advocates for their own programs. This is as it should be. Every teacher should be absolutely convinced that his subject is an integral part of a whole, and that all of the subjects, taken together, amount to a complete, rounded curriculum. The physics teacher knows how important it is for his students to know physics. The art teacher knows that his subject is necessary to a well-rounded curriculum. When the physics department needs new equipment, that is as important to the physics teachers and students as new choral risers are to the music department. When the art program needs new textbooks, that is as important to the art program as new general music texts are to the music program.

Advocacy should not be carried out in a competitive way. Speaking for one's own program should be done in the context of making a meaningful contribution to the whole. The best situation is a win-win agreement: the chemistry department puts off buying some of the new microscopes it needs so there will be enough money for musical instruments, with the understanding that the music department will postpone some of its purchases until the chemistry department has what it needs. A good motto for advocates is, "When you need a friend, it's too late to get a friend."

Questions, Topics and Activities for Critical Thinking

1. Observe and then interview one elementary and one secondary music teacher to learn the procedures, rules and consequences for the music classroom. Create a chart that illustrates the rules and consequences, and make any changes that you feel would be desirable for your own classroom.
2. Locate an article in the *Music Educators Journal* or *Teaching Music* that addresses behavior management in the music classroom, and share with your classmates one or two strategies that you think would be effective.
3. Interview an experienced music teacher and ask for specific procedures on how he handles the music budget, how music is purchased, and how tours are organized. Inquire about other business matters that the teacher found difficult at the beginning of his teaching career.

4. Investigate your state's teacher standards and licensing requirements, including recommendations for portfolio construction. Draft your first professional portfolio.

5. Using resources on music technology listed at the end of this chapter, or others recommended by your professor, select a topic to explore, such as recording and burning a CD of a school ensemble; arranging and printing a professional-looking musical score; practicing sight-reading, ear-training, listening, improvising or composing skills with CAI; adding sound files to websites; or creating an electronic portfolio. Present evidence of your exploration to the class.

6. Look up MENC's advocacy materials on the web (www.menc.org) and discuss whether you would be likely to use them, rather than advocating on the basis of your own experience. If you would use any of the MENC materials, which ones would you select?

Advocacy Readings

"Advocacy and the Music Educator" (position statement). MENC: available http://www.menc.org/about/view/advocacy-and-the-music-educator-position-statement. Available also http://www.menc.org/resources/view/why-music-psa-for-back-to-school-2008.

Americans for the Arts. Available http://www.americansforthearts.org/.

Kennedy Center Alliance for Arts Education. *Schools, Communities, and the Arts: A Research Compendium*. Available www.kennedy-center.org/education/kcaaen.

Mark, Michael L. "A History of Music Education Advocacy." *Music Educators Journal*, September 2002.

MENC publishes numerous materials (books, pamphlets, kits) to support advocacy efforts. Available http://www.menc.org.

Rockefeller, David, Jr. (1979). *Coming to Our Senses: The Significance of Art for American Education*. The Arts, Education and Americans Panel. New York: McGraw-Hill.

Readings

Bauer, William I. (May 2001). "Classroom Management for Ensembles." *Music Educators Journal*, 27–32.

Campbell, D.M., P.B. Cignetti, B.J. Melenyzer, D.H. Nettles & R.M. Wyman (1999). *Portfolio and Performance Assessment in Teacher Education*. Boston, MA: Allyn and Bacon.

—— (2006). *How to Develop a Professional Portfolio: A Manual for Teachers*, 4th ed. Boston: Allyn and Bacon.

Collins, Don L. (1999). *Teaching Choral Music*, 2nd ed. Upper Saddle River, NJ: Prentice Hall.

Criswell, Chad (November 2008). "What Web 2.0 mean for Teachers." *Teaching Music, 16*(3), 24–25.

Gilbert, Nina (May 2005). "Virtual Roundtable Part II: More Advice from Choir Tour Professionals." *Choral Journal, 45*(10), 37–54.

Hansen, Dee (2002). *Handbook for Music Supervision*. Reston, VA: MENC.

Interstate New Teacher Assessment and Support Consortium (INTASC) (1992). *Model Standards for Beginning Teacher Licensing, Assessment and Development: A Resource for State Dialogue*. Washington, DC: Council of Chief State School Officers.

—— (June 2002). *Model Standards for Licensing Classroom Teachers and Specialists in the Arts: A Resource for State Dialogue*. Washington, DC: Council of Chief State School Officers.

Johnson, Ruth S., J. Sabrina Mims-Cox & Adelaide Doyle-Nichols (2006). *Developing Portfolios in Education: A Guide to Reflection, Inquiry, and Assessment*. Thousand Oaks, CA: Sage.

Kersten, Fred (2004). "E-Portfolio for the Internet Job Hunt." *Teaching Music, 1*(4), 40–47.

Madura Ward-Steinman, Patrice (2010). *Becoming a Choral Music Teacher: A Field Experience Workbook*. New York: Routledge.

Moore, Marvelene C. (2002). *Classroom Management in General, Choral and Instrumental Music Programs*. Reston, VA: MENC.

Music Booster Manual (1989, reprinted 1994, 1998). Reston, VA: MENC.

Phillips, Kenneth H. (2004). *Directing the Choral Music Program*. New York: Oxford.

Queen, J. Allen, B.B. Blackwelder & L.P. Mallen (1997). *Responsible Classroom Management for Teachers and Students*. Upper Saddle River, NJ: Prentice Hall.

Rolheiser, C., B. Bower & L. Stevahn (2000). *The Portfolio Organizer: Succeeding with Portfolios in Your Classroom*. Alexandria, VA: Association for Supervision and Curriculum Development.

Rossman, R.L. (1989). *Tips: Discipline in the Music Classroom*. Reston, VA: MENC.

Scarlett, W. George, Iris Chin Ponte & Jay P. Singh (2009). *Approaches to Behavior and Classroom Management*. Thousand Oaks, CA: Sage.

Travel Issue (February 2005), *Choral Journal*, *45*(7), 9–85.

Vartanian, Tina-Marie (2003). "The Need for Mentors: A Survey of First Year Instrumental Music Teachers in Los Angeles and Orange Counties" (Doctoral Dissertation, University of Southern California, 2002). UMI 3094377.

Wiehe, Pat (Spring 2008). "The Functions and Value of a Show Choir Parent Organization." *Resound*, 9–10.

Williams, David Brian & Peter Richard Webster (2008). *Experiencing Music Technology*, Updated 3rd ed. Boston, MA: Schirmer Glengage Learning.

Wong, Harry K. & Rosemary T. Wong (1998). *The First Days of School: How To Be An Effective Teacher*. Mountain View, CA: Harry K. Wong Publications, Inc. (www.effectiveteaching.com).

Wyatt, Robert L. & Sandra Looper (2004). *So You Have to Have a Portfolio: A Teacher's Guide to Preparation and Presentation*, 2nd ed. Thousand Oaks, CA: Corwin Press.

ten
Statements
of Belief

Words that Guide the Profession

FIGURE 10.1 **Nick playing the mellophone**

Dr. Jenkins   When you're a music teacher, you'll do your work in classrooms and rehearsal rooms. But your influence on students, colleagues, and the community will extend beyond the school's walls. This will be made clear to you when you've read what music education leaders have said about teaching music—why music is important to students, the school, and the community; how music education serves communities; how music education has evolved over the years as society has changed. These important documents might be below your radar right now, but when you're into your career you'll appreciate how significant they are.

Nick   Why do I need to know all that? I just want to get into my rehearsal room and get the band ready for concerts and the football season.

Dr. Jenkins   You're right, Nick. You don't need to know all that to be a band director. You don't need it just to teach general music or start beginners on violin or direct a Mariachi ensemble. But you and everyone else in this class will be members of a profession that's important even beyond the walls of the school. You'll contribute to the lives of your students in a way that will help prepare them to be participating and productive citizens. You'll contribute to the cultural and recreational life of your community. You'll be part of the nation's efforts to support its culture. That's a lot of responsibility. Think about it—would music education even exist if it wasn't important to society? You need to know how your work will carry over beyond the rehearsal room and school, even beyond the community. That's why it's important to look at the broader picture of the music education profession.

Nick   And all that begins in my rehearsal hall? Isn't that stretching things?

Dr. Jenkins   I understand why you feel that way, but it's the real thing. Music teachers are very busy people, whether they teach kindergartners or college students. I was well into my career before I found time to really think things through. I knew there have been music teachers for thousands of years, but I didn't know why. It didn't occur to me that if all they did was give young people a fun experience, that would be too shallow to justify the cost. Music has to offer something unique, something that no other activity can provide. We have to respect the uniqueness of music and its place in the curriculum.

Think about it: education changes people. It makes them aware of things that they wouldn't know without an education. It makes them able to do things they couldn't do without an education. Education makes people complete, and music is an important part of education. Education benefits individuals, and individuals together make up communities and the nation. A well-educated citizen is an asset to the community and the nation. But citizens aren't well educated without music, so you, the music teacher, have an important role in the country's quality of life. It's not a stretch—it's real.

Music education has thrived throughout Western history, but our focus right now is on recent times, when music education leaders have paused to step back and look deeply into whether their beliefs and practices still fulfill society's needs. The first two documents that follow are early views of the purpose of music education. See how they compare with later statements. The next three are the summaries of symposia. The complete reports of each symposium are published in book form and are available for you to read. Look at them in your school's music library. The statements are meant to give the music teacher a broad view and appreciation of his or her profession; they're not meant to assist the teacher in the classroom the next day.

Notice that all of the statements are published by the umbrella organization of the music education profession, MENC. They are expressions of belief that influence the entire music education profession. The specialized organizations other than MENC that focus on specific areas of music education are necessary and valuable, but MENC is the only organization that embraces every professional interest. In fact, every school subject has a national professional umbrella organization. English, physical education, social studies—and all the other subjects—have their own equivalents of MENC.

A Declaration of Faith, Purpose and Action[1]

These resolutions were adopted by the Music Educators National Conference, Cleveland, on April 1, 1946. This declaration is a broad statement of belief in the value of music education when the nation was beginning to return to normal after the difficult years of World War II. Its focus is broad, with emphasis on the role of music education in the national context.

We, the members of the Music Educators National Conference, reaffirm our conviction that music is a beneficent agent for making life more satisfying. In peace as well as in war, music is one of the most important sources of spiritual sustenance ...

We believe in America; we believe that music is helping to strengthen the power and ideals of our country. We believe it is our responsibility to bend every effort to the end that this power of music shall reach into the whole life of America, through every community, and contribute its full share to our national welfare and development ...

Music Teaching as an Exponent of Democratic Processes. While we are training thousands of young men for military duty, we must also train the younger millions to embrace the ideals and democratic processes for which civilization strives. To that end each one of us is under the necessity of searching out procedures of teaching that will make our classroom the highest example of a functioning democracy.

The Broadening Scope of Musical Experiences. Lines of separation between popular entertainment music, on the one hand, and the music of standard concert and opera repertoires, on the other, are slowly but surely becoming less marked ...

Both the so-called popular and so-called high-brow music of today stem from the cultural level of this period of our national growth, and in music, as elsewhere, we are a nation uneasy in our diversity of contrasts.

It follows that bases of judgment and choice of values for our young people are the more imperative. We, therefore, recommend that music educators seriously study ways and means of achieving a combination of the dynamic factors embodied in the music of today and the enduring music of the past in programs that remain consistent with the aims of music education.

International Cultural Relations Through Music. A world at peace is the dearest hope of the millions of people in every country on earth. Music is the universal language and should be utilized at its highest potential power to help win and sustain world-wide peace.

We, the members of the Music Educators National Conference, therefore, urge the adoption of the bill now pending before Congress authorizing the cooperation of the United States in the United Nations Educational, Scientific and Cultural Organizations ...

Providing Music Material is a Social Responsibility. Since the foundations of democracy are rooted in broad education, the providing of material for the educational process is a matter of public concern. Music Education is highly dependent upon adequate variety of books, music, instruments, records, and other aids, many of which cannot equal in sales the figures reached by purely entertainment products.

The Tanglewood Declaration[2]

The decade of the 1960s was a time of civil unrest in the United States. The Civil Rights revolution and the war in Viet Nam led to massive protest demonstrations to bring about change in the nation's laws and policies and its involvement in an unpopular war. It was also a decade of emerging technology, when computers began to affect the lives of ordinary people in ways they had not imagined before. Social change was occurring at a faster pace than ever before and music educators realized that their profession needed to change as well to keep up with societal needs. Thus, the Tanglewood Symposium. The Symposium was held at Tanglewood, Massachusetts in the summer of 1967 to evaluate the role of music education in a time of rapid societal change.

The Declaration's second recommendation was the most relevant and the one that affected the profession the most: "Music of all periods, styles, forms, and cultures belongs in the curriculum." It came about during the Civil Rights revolution, when Americans demanded that all people deserved and needed to be treated equally by law and by custom. This simple, declarative sentence was the basis for the adoption of all kinds of music in the curriculum. For the first time, the profession blessed the adoption of jazz, folk music, popular music, and any and all ethnic musics. During the next few years, some music educators became knowledgeable of other kinds of music than that of the Western European tradition. Books, texts, recordings, and other teaching materials became available, and eventually, multicultural musics became a standard part of the music curriculum throughout the United States. It is interesting to note that the day after the Tanglewood Declaration was released, the National Association of Jazz Educators was created. It eventually became the International Association of Jazz Educators, which existed until 2008.

The fifth recommendation, "Developments in educational technology, educational television, programmed instruction, and computer-assisted instruction should be applied to music study and research," also proved to be a critical turning point for the profession. Personal computers were in their earliest stages at that time, as were synthesizers that were inexpensive and small enough to be used in schools. Electronic equipment is commonplace now in music classrooms and rehearsal halls, and it can be traced back to the Tanglewood Declaration.

The other recommendations also led to important changes that helped music educators keep current with the needs of American society. These things did not happen immediately. Gradually, in an organized manner, changes occurred.

The intensive evaluation of the role of music in American society and education provided by the Tanglewood Symposium of philosophers, educators, scientists, labor leaders, philanthropists, social scientists, theologians, industrialists, representatives of government and foundations, music educators and other musicians led to this declaration:

> We believe that education must have as major goals the art of living, the building of personal identity, and nurturing creativity. Since the study of music can contribute much to these ends, we now call for music to be placed in the core of the school curriculum.
>
> The arts afford a continuity with the aesthetic tradition in man's history. Music and other fine arts, largely non-verbal in nature, reach close to the social, psychological, and physiological roots of man in his search for identity and self-realization.
>
> Educators must accept the responsibility for developing opportunities which meet man's individual needs and the needs of a society plagued by the consequences of changing values, alienation, hostility between generations, racial and international tensions, and the challenges of a new leisure.

Music educators at Tanglewood agreed on the following:

1. Music serves best when its integrity as an art is maintained.
2. Music of all periods, styles, forms, and cultures belongs in the curriculum. The musical repertory should be expanded to involve music of our time in its rich variety, including currently popular teenage music and avant-garde music, American folk music, and the music of other cultures.
3. Schools and colleges should provide adequate time for music in programs ranging from preschool through adult or continuing education.
4. Instruction in the arts should be a general and important part of education in the senior high school.
5. Developments in educational technology, educational television, programmed instruction, and computer-assisted instruction should be applied to music study and research.
6. Greater emphasis should be placed on helping the individual student to fulfill his needs, goals and potentials.
7. The music education profession must contribute its skills, proficiencies, and insights toward assisting in the solution of urgent social problems as in the "inner city" or other areas with culturally deprived individuals.

8. Programs of teacher education must be expanded and improved to provide music teachers who are specially equipped to teach high school courses in the history and literature of music, courses in the humanities and related arts, as well as teachers equipped to work with the very young, with adults, with the disadvantaged, and with the emotionally disturbed.

Growing Up Complete: The Imperative for Music Education[3]

Growing Up Complete was written in 1991, at a time when music educators were concerned that their subject was in danger of losing its place in the curriculum.

A Declaration of Concern. During the 1960s, education reform made it onto the front pages of American newspapers for the first time in decades. Politicians, policy makers, and business figures have been quick to trace the nation's "competitiveness gap" to the schoolhouse door. They have voiced ringing alarms over the declines in math and science scores. But when the discussion has turned to making sure our children learn to understand and participate in music and the other arts, there has been silence. We believe such nearsighted concern shortchanges our children because it leaves them only half-educated. Since the beginnings of civilization, music has been universally recognized as crucial to quality education, for two reasons.

First, every civilization recognizes that both formal and informal music education prepare children for what life ultimately requires. Music education fosters creativity, provides basic tools for a critical assessment of the world around us, and instills the abiding values of self-discipline and commitment.

Second, music and the other arts have been recognized as unique to human capabilities, as a means to self-discovery and self-expression, and as a fundamental part of civilization itself.

We, whose lives are marked indelibly by a love for music, and who understand the essential role music education can play in developing the whole human being, call on the parents of our school children, on teachers and school officials, on local and state boards of education, and on the American people, to come to our aid in establishing the rightful place of music in the schools.

Our credo is simple: Just as there can be no music without learning, no education is complete without music. Music makes the difference. To that end:

We call on all who care about education to destroy, once and for all, the myth that education in music and the other arts is mere "curricular icing";

We call on all who love the arts to insist that instruction in music and the other arts be reestablished as basic to education, not only by virtue of their intrinsic worth, but because they are fundamental to what it means to be an educated person;

We call on parents, educators, and citizens who know and understand the value of music in our common life to bring the message about the value of music education to decision makers at all levels, and to encourage them to establish music as a priority, so our children can continue to learn and make music; and

We call on those whose livelihoods depend on music—as manufacturers, technicians, teachers, retailers, performers, composers, and others—to lend their support to the cause of music education in our schools ...

Education with Music. What is true of all the arts is supremely true of music. When a child studies music, significant elements of his or her education find focus and expression:

- developing the ability to understand and use symbols in new contexts;
- discovering the power, precision, and control of mathematics in unexpected ways;
- finding and directing personal creativity;
- exercising the diverse skills of problem-solving;
- experiencing the joy of self-expression;
- growing into the liberation acquired through self-discipline; and
- participating in the deeply human satisfaction of shared work and the gratification of challenges met.

In addition to these characteristics fundamental to education, music shares with the other arts a resource that is of paramount importance to the education of the young: Music is a highway for exploring the emotional and aesthetic dimensions of experience. Indeed, here is where music and the other arts make their unique and most visible contribution. Education *without* music shortchanges our children and their futures. Education *with* music offers exciting possibilities in two directions. As we look to the future, educational research on the nature of intelligence and brain function give promising indications that could change the face of education. And as we look around us in the present, we see connections between music education and changes in students that offer direct and immediate benefits, not only to them, but to the educational enterprise as a whole.

The National Education Standards[4]

The National Education Standards originated in 1990, when Congress passed the Goals 2000: Educate America Act. The Act was intended to frame education reform throughout the nation; ensure equitable educational opportunities for all students; provide a framework for reauthorization of all Federal education programs; and create a voluntary national system of skill standards and certifications. National standards for several subjects were created in 1994.

MENC had advocated for the standards as part of the Consortium of National Arts Education Associations (music, art, drama, and dance education). When the Goals 2000: Educate America Act was passed, the arts were recognized for the first time as a fundamental academic subject. Paul Lehman, then President of MENC, wrote:

The standards project has given arts educators control of the agenda in the debate over arts education. It has enabled arts educators to lead the discussion.

This was not the case previously. In past years, for example, initiatives in arts education were routinely taken by advocacy groups or other organizations with no competence or experience in arts education, and not surprisingly, nothing worthwhile or permanent happened. But now MENC has seized the initiative and has proven that it's a major force on the Washington scene. Don't underestimate the significance of that achievement.

(Lehman 1994)

In 1994, teams of leaders of each of the arts disciplines developed national standards for grades K–12. The standards describe the knowledge, skills, and understanding that all students should acquire in the arts and are a basis for developing curricula. Following that, the states developed their own standards for each subject. Some states require the standards to be implemented in the schools and they are voluntary in other states.

Summary statement: What students should know and be able to do in the arts. There are many routes to competence in the arts disciplines. Students may work in different arts at different times. Their study may take a variety of approaches. Their abilities may develop at different rates. Competence means the ability to use an array of knowledge and skills. Terms often used to describe these include creation, performance, production, history, culture, perception, analysis, criticism, aesthetics, technology, and appreciation. Competence means capabilities with these elements themselves and an understanding of their interdependence; it also means the ability to combine the content, perspectives, and techniques associated with the various elements to achieve specific artistic and analytical goals. Students work toward comprehensive competence from the very beginning, preparing in the lower grades for deeper and more rigorous work each succeeding year. As a result, the joy of experiencing the arts is enriched and matured by the discipline of learning and the pride of accomplishment. Essentially, the Standards ask that students should know and be able to do the following by the time they have completed secondary school:

- They should be able to communicate at a basic level in the four arts disciplines dance, music, theatre, and the visual arts. This includes knowledge and skills in the use of the basic vocabularies, materials, tools, techniques, and intellectual methods of each arts discipline.
- They should be able to communicate proficiently in at least one art form, including the ability to define and solve artistic problems with insight, reason, and technical proficiency.
- They should be able to develop and present basic analyses of works of art from structural, historical, and cultural perspectives, and from combinations of those perspectives. This includes the ability to understand and evaluate work in the various arts disciplines.
- They should have an informed acquaintance with exemplary works of art from a variety of cultures and historical periods, and a basic understanding of historical development in the arts disciplines, across the arts as a whole, and within cultures.

- They should be able to relate various types of arts knowledge and skills within and across the arts disciplines. This includes mixing and matching competencies and understandings in art-making, history and culture, and analysis in any arts-related project.

As a result of developing these capabilities, students can arrive at their own knowledge, beliefs, and values for making personal and artistic decisions. In other terms, they can arrive at a broad-based, well-grounded understanding of the nature, value, and meaning of the arts as a part of their own humanity.

These National Standards for Arts Education are a statement of what every young American should know and be able to do in four arts disciplines: dance, music, theatre, and the visual arts. Their scope is grades K–12, and they speak to both content and achievement.

National Standards for Music Education
1. Singing, alone and with others, a varied repertoire of music.
2. Performing on instruments, alone and with others, a varied repertoire of music.
3. Improvising melodies, variations, and accompaniments.
4. Composing and arranging music within specified guidelines.
5. Reading and notating music.
6. Listening to, analyzing, and describing music.
7. Evaluating music and music performances.
8. Understanding relationships between music, the other arts, and disciplines outside the arts.
9. Understanding music in relation to history and culture.

Vision 2020: The Housewright Declaration[5]

Vision 2020, the Housewright Symposium on the Future of Music Education was held at the Florida State University, Tallahassee, in September, 1999. It was named after Dr. Wiley Housewright, former president of MENC and Dean of the School of Music of Florida State University. The purpose of the symposium was to set a vision for the music education profession for the next 20 years, to the year 2020. Society had changed as it progressed technologically and in civil rights since the Tanglewood Symposium of 32 years earlier, and the symposium's organizers, led by MENC president June Hinckley, recognized that it was time for another professional introspection.

The summary document, the Housewright Declaration, was more personal and philosophical than the Tanglewood Declaration. It discusses the effect of music on individuals in greater depth. The statement reflects contemporary issues like music teacher recruitment and education as well as new roles and responsibilities of music educators. It is a visionary statement that confirms the ideas and suggestions of the Tanglewood Declaration of three decades earlier.

Whenever and wherever humans have existed music has existed also. Since music occurs only when people choose to create and share it, and since they always have done so and no doubt always will, music clearly must have important value for people.

Music makes a difference in people's lives. It exalts the human spirit; it enhances the quality of life. Indeed, meaningful music activity should be experienced throughout one's life toward the goal of continuing involvement.

Music is a basic way of knowing and doing because of its own nature and because of the relationship of that nature to the human condition, including mind, body, and feeling. It is worth studying because it represents a basic mode of thought and action, and because in itself, it is one of the primary ways human beings create and share meanings. It must be studied fully to access this richness.

Societal and technological changes will have an enormous impact for the future of music education. Changing demographics and increased technological advancements are inexorable and will have profound influences on the ways that music is experienced for both students and teachers.

Music educators must build on the strengths of current practice to take responsibility for charting the future of music education to insure that the best of the Western art tradition and other musical traditions are transmitted to future generations. We agree on the following:

1. All persons, regardless of age, cultural heritage, ability, venue, or financial circumstance deserve to participate fully in the best music experiences possible.
2. The integrity of music study must be preserved. Music educators must lead the development of meaningful music instruction and experience.
3. Time must be allotted for formal music study at all levels of instruction such that a comprehensive, sequential and standards based program of music instruction is made available.
4. All music has a place in the curriculum. Not only does the Western art tradition need to be preserved and disseminated, music educators also need to be aware of other music that people experience and be able to integrate it into classroom music instruction.
5. Music educators need to be proficient and knowledgeable concerning technological changes and advancements and be prepared to use all appropriate tools in advancing music study while recognizing the importance of people coming together to make and share music.
6. Music educators should involve the music industry, other agencies, individuals, and music institutions in improving the quality and quantity of music instruction. This should start within each local community by defining the appropriate role of these resources in teaching and learning.
7. The currently defined role of the music educator will expand as settings for music instruction proliferate. Professional music educators must provide a leadership role in coordinating music activities beyond the school setting to insure formal and informal curricular integration.
8. Recruiting prospective music teachers is a responsibility of many, including music educators. Potential teachers need to be drawn from diverse back-

grounds, identified early, led to develop both teaching and musical abilities, and sustained through ongoing professional development. Also, alternative licensing should be explored in order to expand the number and variety of teachers available to those seeking music instruction.

9. Continuing research addressing all aspects of music activity needs to be supported including intellectual, emotional, and physical responses to music. Ancillary social results of music study also need exploration as well as specific studies to increase meaningful music listening.
10. Music making is an essential way in which learners come to know and understand music and music traditions. Music making should be broadly interpreted to be performing, composing, improvising, listening, and interpreting music notation.
11. Music educators must join with others in providing opportunities for meaningful music instruction for all people beginning at the earliest possible age and continuing throughout life.
12. Music educators must identify the barriers that impede the full actualization of any of the above and work to overcome them.

A Centennial Declaration of MENC: The National Association for Music Education[6]

MENC, founded in 1907 in Keokuk, Iowa, celebrated its centennial anniversary in 2007. One of its celebratory events was the Centennial Congress: "Meeting the Goals of Music Education." The attendees were members of the MENC National Assembly (national and state music education officers). The event concluded with the writing of "A Centennial Declaration." This declaration is more specific about the needs of the music education profession than the two previous declarations. The declaration begins with a statement that reaffirms the basic ideas of the previous declarations, and goes on to identify problems and issues, and specific needs of the profession. It discusses these matters in greater detail than the other declarations. It is also the only one of the three to discuss advocacy, which had become a major activity of the profession by the early 1970s.

The Congress focused on two topics:

1. *Our shared goals for music education.* For decades, the broad education community has been in agreement with the music education community on the importance of music education for every child in America. We need to review and renew this agreement in light of current trends in education and society.
2. *Why, in light of our longstanding agreement on goals, music education is not yet universal.* Even without strong, exact data on the status of music education programs around the nation, it seems clear that some large percentage of American children—estimates hover around half of the total population—do not receive a credible music education.

We are in agreement that the basic ideals long expressed by the music education profession and other education professionals are still current: It is the right of every child to receive a balanced, comprehensive, sequential music education taught by qualified music teachers.

A healthy society requires musically fulfilled people. The primary purpose of education is not to create a workforce; it is to improve the quality of life for individuals and for society. Although music education has been valued throughout history for its unique contributions, it is not yet universal in American schools. Serious problems persist, including inequality of access, uneven quality of programs, and insufficient valuing of music as a part of the curriculum. As a result, music is often pushed to the periphery of the school experience. In this centennial year of 2007, we reaffirm our longstanding ideals in a challenging context that calls for directed action in curriculum, assessment, research, teacher education, advocacy, and building alliances.

Needs Regarding Curriculum. Our curriculum must reflect more than our own desires; it must reflect the needs and desires of the students we serve. We seek contexts and modes of instruction that will provide students with more inclusive experiences of the styles and genres of music and the many musical roles that are practiced in our society and that are represented in the national content standards. We need to develop programs that are flexible and of greater variety than those currently in use in most schools. This will require efforts including identifying and promulgating effective models, rethinking teacher education, expanding inservice development opportunities, and developing new assessment techniques. These initiatives necessitate an expansion of our research interests and a greater application of research results in teacher education programs and in classrooms. We need to develop deeper insight into the role of music in general education, focusing on what is distinctive about music and on its complementary relationship to other subjects. We need electives as broad and diverse as the interests and enthusiasms of our students.

Needs Regarding Assessment. We need assessment techniques and strategies that are suited to the domain of music in all its complexity and diversity. We need to focus our energies on the development of multiple assessment strategies that reflect the dimensions of students' musical growth and draw upon a broad range of instructional methodologies and techniques. We need assessment criteria that go beyond attendance, effort, and attitude. We need formative assessments of students' learning—including portfolios and other techniques, and we need program evaluations based on the Opportunity to Learn Standards.

Needs Regarding Advocacy. We need to arrive at ways to transmit a uniform message to decision makers and to the public. We need strong alliances with those who share or understand the value of music study and are willing to join with us in advocating for strong, vibrant music programs. We need to make advocacy efforts that clarify and celebrate the enhanced opportunities to learn that we are striving to make available.

Toward the Future. We will build on our first hundred years of success with a second century of leadership and service. Our musical culture, our students, and our society deserve no less.

The Authors' Beliefs

Michael L. Mark

FIGURE 10.2 **Michael L. Mark**

Music educators fulfill a role in society that is not duplicated by any other kind of teacher. History tells us that the significance of their work to young people and to society has always been respected and valued by society, and there is every reason to believe it will continue into the future. Since music education was first introduced as a curricular subject in 1838, it has influenced the lives of countless Americans who, as mature, productive citizens, fulfill a significant role in helping the United States become one of the most advanced nations in human history.

As the schools prepare each student for a productive adult citizenship, the impact of music education is felt in larger settings—the school band, orchestra, chorus, the community, the nation. This broad view of the role of music education acknowledges that the country has need of musically educated citizens. The greatness of American culture lies in large part in its music, and nations are respected for their cultures. Music teachers will always be needed to educate young people about their American culture and the numerous heritages that come together to form the United States of America.

As society changes and advances, so does music education. Music teachers have always recognized the societal needs that determine their role, and they have always adapted with creative ways of teaching and with appropriate music.

There have been difficult times for music programs in the history of American music education, always related to lack of sufficient resources. Yet, music education has not only survived, but flourished. This phenomenon occurs when the national economy falters, but the American public recognizes the intrinsic importance of music to the individual and to society. It acknowledges the importance of music in the schools. The public has repeatedly insisted that music programs continue despite difficult economic times. Over and over, the public has demonstrated that it could not afford to not have music in its schools. It would be instructive to read the Dana Foundation's *Arts Education* (March 2009). It contains several articles about how arts education remains strong in schools and communities during a time of economic difficulty (www.dana.org).

Change is a theme that runs throughout this book. Change in society, change in music education. Change is a constant in today's world, and music education students must be ready to adapt in order to remain relevant as they take their places in the schools. They will need to become skillful in discussing their music programs and presenting their needs convincingly to decision makers. They will need to read professional journals, speak to their colleagues in other schools, participate in their professional associations, and educate their communities and boards of education to the essential nature of music in education. They will need to take graduate level courses and degrees that will advance them professionally. And they will need to continue to be inspired by music as they do their daily work of inspiring their students with the joy of music.

We believe that music educators will continue to serve the students of the United States. We admire, value, and appreciate the music educators who are charged with enriching the lives of our young people by advancing our music culture and passing it on to future generations.

Patrice Madura

Every music educator must decide what beliefs will guide them throughout their professional life. We have all had different musical and educational experiences, resulting in different values. We are individuals who bring our own special talents to the music world. Yet, despite our differences, we all have some special things in common.

We have studied music and through our experiences and achievements have had peak experiences that have motivated us to continue to study music. We have learned discipline and perseverance through our music study, and we have valued our musical abilities because they allow us to express ourselves in times of sadness, frustration, joy and triumph.

We also have an affinity for education. We have been inspired by our music teachers, and know that they have helped us find meaning in our lives. We want to inspire others

FIGURE 10.3 **Patrice Madura Ward-Steinman**

as our teachers inspired us. We believe that a career combining the arts of music and teaching is an ideal one. The fact that we can continue to perform as well as lead our students in performances that inspire audience members are also deciding factors. These are all worthy reasons to become a music teacher.

But we need to dig a little deeper to realize that because we are fortunate to be music educators we also have important responsibilities to the future musical well-being of our students, our schools, our nation, and the human race. We need to reflect on the deeper meanings of a musical education, and chart our course with our beliefs. Our beliefs are based on our upbringing and education, which color our values regarding the standards and expectations of our profession. This is because we teach best what we know and love most. The things I know and love best are the piano, the singing voice, the great masterworks of Bach through Berio, vocal and instrumental jazz, and nostalgically, some rock and folk music of the 1960s. These are the things I am most enthusiastic about teaching and performing. And of course you have your favorites.

Along with our favorites, we have a responsibility as world citizens to understand other cultures. I have learned much about other cultures through my studies of African-American jazz and gospel music, of Balinese and Javanese gamelan, of Brazilian samba and bossa nova, and of Irish mouth music. I believe the study of these world musics opens our minds and hearts to people of other cultures, and so we must learn and teach others to be multi-musical.

I also believe that the masterworks of the Western classical music tradition are a treasure and we have a responsibility to pass the understanding of these on to the next generation of students. If we don't teach the music of Bach, Mozart, Haydn, Beethoven, Brahms, Debussy, Bartok and Stravinsky, who will? It would be unheard of to teach visual art and not present the great works of Rembrandt, Monet, Renoir, Van Gogh and Picasso. These works have stood the test of time and reveal great depth, mastery, and indeed mystery of art. We can be confident that our choirs, bands, orchestras, chamber ensembles and soloists will live on, as will our audiences, because of the vitality and importance of these works.

On the other hand, I believe that there is more to music study than the performance of composed works. It is the creative activity of music, whether through improvisation or composition, that can be the most engaging musical experience of all. Improvisation and composition allow the personal expression that can motivate a student to remain involved in and value music for a lifetime.

In time, research will reveal whether music instruction and participation really do make one smarter or enhance other academic, social, psychological or physical skills. When more research evidence is found, we can use those findings to convince those who need convincing that music is important to education. But we musicians know that music makes a difference in people's lives, whether they are young children or senior citizens, and in order to bring more goodwill to this world, there will always be a need for music teachers to guide the next generation of musicians. Believe in what you do. It is an honorable profession.

Questions, Topics and Activities for Critical Thinking

1. *A Declaration of Faith, Purpose and Action*
   Look over the topics in this declaration and analyze whether they are relevant to today's music education. What specific points relate to what you remember from your high school music program?
2. *The Tanglewood Symposium*
   Discuss why it was so important in 1967 that the music education profession officially approved the use of multicultural musics, jazz, popular music, folk music, and other kinds of music. What recommendations of the Tanglewood Declaration are especially important in today's music education?
3. *Growing Up Complete: The Imperative for Music Education*
   To whom do you think this piece is directed? Music educators? The public? Do you believe it is persuasive during a time when resources for schools are scarce?

4. *The National Education Standards*

   Looking back at your own high school music experiences, were all of the nine standards included in your program? If not, which ones were?

5. *Vision 2020: The Housewright Declaration*

   Discuss the similarities and differences in the Tanglewood Declaration and the Housewright Declaration.

6. *A Centennial Declaration of MENC: The National Association for Music Education*

   To whom do you think the Centennial Declaration is directed? Do you think it is persuasive to decision makers and the general public?

7. Each of the documents was sponsored by MENC. Why? Is it possible that they might have been sponsored by other organizations? Which organizations?

8. Which of the documents do you believe to be the most relevant for the music education profession?

9. Which of the documents is most relevant for you in regard to your particular interests?

10. Are there any questions or statements in the documents that you disagree with? Which ones? Why do you disagree?

11. Do you consider any or all of the documents to be backward looking? Forward looking? Visionary?

Readings

Centennial Declaration: available http://menc.org/about/view/centennial-declaration.

Choate, Robert A., ed. (1968). *Documentary Report of the Tanglewood Symposium*. Washington, DC: Music Educators National Conference.

Dana Foundation (March 2009). *Arts Education*. www.dana.org/artseducation.aspx.

Lehman, Paul (1994). "The National Standards: From Vision to Reality." *Music Educators Journal*, 58(2), special insert.

Madsen, Clifford, ed. (2000). *Vision 2020: The Housewright Symposium on the Future of Music Education*. Reston, VA: Music Educators National Conference.

Mark, Michael L. (1996). *Contemporary Music Education*, 3rd ed. New York: Schirmer. See pp. 38–45 (Tanglewood Symposium) and pp. 45–48 (The Goals and Objectives Project).

—— (2008). *Music Education: Source Readings from Ancient Greece to Today*, 3rd ed. New York: Routledge.

Morgan, Hazel Nohavec, ed. (1947). *Music Education Source Book*. Chicago, IL: Music Educators National Conference, xi–xii.

National Commission on Music Education (1991). "Education with Music." In *Growing Up Complete: The Imperative for Music Education*. Reston, VA: MENC. Copyright © 1991 Music Educators National Conference. Reprinted with permission. Available http://menc.org/about/view/centennial-declaration, http://menc.org/gp/search?data[collection]=site-search&q=music+standards. See this site for a listing of MENC publications about performance standards for many music education areas based on the National Standards for Music.

Vision 2020: The Housewright Symposium on the Future of Music Education (2000). Reston, VA: MENC.

eleven
Preparing for the Future of Music Education

FIGURE 11.1 **African drum and dance ensemble**

Twenty-first Century Skills

As the United States continues to evolve as a highly technological and informational society, its education system must evolve as well. The challenges of the 21st century are different from those of earlier times, and educators need to consider what knowledge and skills their students will need as they take their places as adults in 21st century society. The Partnership for 21st Century Skills (www.21stcenturyskills.org), a group of more than 30 education organizations, policy makers, manufacturers, and technology and media companies, proposes a vision for student success in the global economy. Its Framework for 21st Century Learning includes four broad outcomes:

- Core Subjects (which include the arts) weaved together with four 21st century interdisciplinary themes
  - Global Awareness
  - Financial, Economic, Business and Entrepreneurial Literacy
  - Civic Literacy
  - Health Literacy
- Learning and Innovation Skills
  - Creativity and Innovation
  - Critical Thinking and Problem Solving
  - Communication and Collaboration
- Information, Media and Technology Skills
  - Information Literacy
  - Media Literacy
  - Communications and Technology Literacy
- Life and Career Skills
  - Flexibility and Adaptability
  - Initiative and Self-direction
  - Social and Cross-cultural Skills
  - Productivity and Accountability
  - Leadership and Responsibility

Music education has a necessary role in preparing students to meet the needs of the 21st century global society. There are implications for education reform paradigms that could make our profession look somewhat different from what it is now if it is to remain relevant to the future. Students will grow up in a different kind of society, and music education must continually adjust to meet their needs. For example, Sir Kenneth Robinson wrote about the need for creativity, "humanity's future depends on our ability to 'reconstitute our conception of human capacity'" (Robinson 2006).

Music, theater, visual arts and dance already incorporate many of the 21st century skills that are identified as essential for success in the new millennium. For example, global awareness is experienced in music classes that teach songs and instrumental pieces from around the world, and these music experiences enlighten students to "the cultural heritage of the human family" (Fowler 1996).

Creativity and innovation are experienced in musical composition and improvisation studies, and critical thinking and problem solving are common to decisions musicians make when rehearsing the technical and expressive details of solos and ensembles (Deturk 2002).

Musicians communicate meaning and values in multiple languages in choral settings; ensemble members collaborate to accomplish common musical goals; and musicians develop technology literacy through sound systems, recording devices, and notation software that are commonly used in their work.

They also develop life skills such as flexibility, goal-management, and independent and self-directed learning as a result of years of disciplined musical study, often alone in a practice room, and/or under pressure to prepare for performances, and with the acceptance of praise, setbacks and criticism that performances and competitions inevitably yield over time. And social skills, leadership, and responsibility are developed as members and section leaders of musical ensembles work together for the benefit of the group.

But there are many aspects of music education that can be improved to better integrate other 21st century skills. The creative skills of improvisation and composition are not yet integral parts of the music curriculum, primarily due to music teachers' lack of adequate training in these skills (Fowler 1996; Madura Ward-Steinman 2007). In addition, teachers can do more to inform their students of health risks such as hearing loss due to exposure to dangerously loud music (Hill 2003) and overuse injuries common to many pianists, violinists and singers (see the journal *Medical Problems of Performing Artists*). Music teachers can do more to provide their students with knowledge of various entrepreneurial career options in the music profession (see Baskerville's *Music Business Handbook and Career Guide*), and to involve them in civic decisions regarding arts advocacy. Students should be expected to communicate in written form their analysis and interpretation of live and recorded music. The creative-thinking music teacher can brainstorm many ways to enrich the music class with 21st century themes and skills.

Fortunately, a collaborative arts organization is working to bring awareness of the key role arts education plays in the development of the 21st century skills of creative thinking. The Arts Education Partnership (AEP) is a national coalition of arts, education, business, philanthropic and government organizations whose primary mission is to build a body of research that explores the role of arts education in the preparation of students for life in the 21st century (www.ccsso.org/projects/Arts_Education_Partnership/). Current research results showing the effectiveness of arts education can be accessed through AEP's website. AEP's book, *Arts Education and 21st Century Learning Research and Policy Agenda*, is an excellent introduction to visionary arts education in the 21st century.

The future of music education is in the hands of the current music education majors. Many will spend their entire careers teaching in the public schools, and others will go on to earn advanced degrees and train future generations of music educators. Awareness of the history, philosophy, psychology, sociology, and pedagogy of music education, combined with musicianship, intelligence, artistry, curiosity, open-mindedness, diligence, ethics, and the desire to continue to learn are just a few of the qualities that need to be nurtured in future teachers. Music education majors also need to be challenged and encouraged to tackle difficult issues with informed actions in preparation for the years ahead.

Keeping Up with New Knowledge

Music education majors are continually exposed to new ideas about teaching and learning music. But in future years, when the teacher is no longer a student taking classes, it will be up to her to stay current. This is most effectively done by keeping membership current in professional organizations, by attending yearly conferences in the area of one's musical specialty or interest, and by regularly reading professional journals and books. It is the new ideas that teachers will read about, and the new ensemble pieces that they will hear at conference concerts and reading sessions that will inspire and motivate them to continue to learn to be better teachers. The teacher should try something new in each class (Conway & Hodgman 2009). Without new ideas we become stuck in our day-to-day routines and eventually begin to feel "burned out." This happens to everyone at one time or another and the antidote is to make the effort to stretch one's self to learn something new, whether through observations of colleagues' teaching, summer workshops, graduate school, or even lessons in something outside of music, such as flying an airplane, travel, cooking, or golf. The result is a more interesting, enthusiastic, and happy person.

Visionary Approaches to the Future

It will be important for future music teachers to think critically about the music education profession's role in society, as well as its strengths and weaknesses in fulfilling its potential. It will be the music educators' responsibility to envision all that music education can be beyond one's own classroom, and collaborate as well as lead others in improving music education. Some topics will be controversial, so the leaders of tomorrow will need to stay informed and be involved. Some provocative visions for music education in the new millennium are discussed below.

FIGURE 11.2 **New Orleans street musicians**

Music Appreciation for All

Questions that music educators might ask themselves are:

- Do we, as a profession, inspire the general public to participate in music all of their lives?
- Do we prepare students with the skills that will transfer to music making for the rest of their lives?
- What kinds of musical participation are the richest and most rewarding?
- Does music appreciation mean primarily music listening for enjoyment, or should appreciation include music making?
- Do we enable all students to learn to enjoy making music in the style or culture of their choice?
- Do we provide students with knowledge of post-secondary musical participation opportunities?
- Can we do a better job of making our nation more musical?
- Is the school music experience more about a technically accurate performance goal or about the special moments of human fulfillment?
- Is the instrument lesson more about technique or about the beauty of a well-played phrase? (Jellison 2000; Regelski 2005; Koopman 2005.)

These are important questions for the future of music education.

Justification for the Arts

The future music educator may be called upon to justify the arts in the schools. In that case, questions regarding which justifications are the most important will need to be reflected upon.

- Should the justifications be based on the effectiveness of music instruction to improve skills in other academic areas, or should they focus on the knowledge of self and of the human condition that musical engagement engenders? (Koopman 2005)
- What is music education's purpose?
- If its purpose is to prepare students to live and create a good life, is collaboration or competition a more enriching goal for music study?

There are no easy answers to these questions, and in fact, the questions themselves may be more important than the answers to music teachers as they envision possibilities for the future.

Improvisation

The Western classical music tradition that permeates university music study does little to promote understanding of improvisation. Yet, within Western classical music history, improvisation was common as it is in various world musics as well as in American pop and jazz idioms. Improvising is a unique musical experience because it requires awareness of the present musical moment, often in collaboration with others similarly engaged. The sense of self-expression and collaboration within the music is deeply gratifying (Lines 2005). Visionary questions arise:

- Should classical music education include improvisation study?
- Should popular and world musics be included in the music curriculum in part because of the improvising skills that can be learned through them?
- Should the non-improvising music teacher seek out music improvisation instruction?

These are only a few questions that the thoughtful music educator of the future might ask.

Digital Technology

While CDs, DVDs, email, iPods, MP3 players, iTunes, CD burners, PowerPoint displays, Facebook, Twitter, blogs, PDFs and distance learning are now part of daily life, there are newer technologies such as Multi-User Virtual Environment (MUVE), Podcast, Video on Demand (Vodcast), wikis, Voice Over Internet Protocol (VoIP), digital TV, peer-to-peer (P2P) network, radio frequency identification technology (RFID) and Smart Cards that provide tremendous opportunities for music teaching (Leong 2007; Nardo 2009).

Music education is likely to change dramatically with the use of emerging technologies. Music educators will need to be informed about and adapt to these new technologies and their use by their students. Important questions will need to be asked by music teachers regarding the relevance of their instruction to increasingly technological youth. There have been criticisms that school music education programs are disconnected from the music technology that students enjoy, resulting in declining enrollments in school music classes (Lamont, et al. 2003; Hodges 2007). Some questions that teachers will need to continue to ask include:

- Should music in the school become more relevant to music outside of school, in light of technological advances?
- Should music study in school be made more applicable to musical interests of the students and the community?
- Should the focus of music instruction in the digital age be on traditional music skills aided by technology, or on discovering new possibilities of sound manipulation with new technologies? (Ruthmann 2007.)
- Does collaborative musical improvisation and composition through networked computers in real time, perhaps even in different countries, provide valuable enhanced creativity opportunities for students? (Brown & Dillon 2007.)
- Should the music curriculum work to offer a diversity of practices in order to be meaningful and enjoyable for the majority of students, rather than an elite few? (Hodges 2007.)

Technology will continue to evolve and music teachers will need to be prepared for a shifting paradigm for music education.

An Increasingly Diverse Nation

Twenty-first century music educators will see changes in demographics to include increasing numbers of culturally diverse students, mobile families, extended families and single parents. The changing society suggests that many more culturally diverse teachers will need to be recruited to represent the "huge minority population explosion" (Spearman 2000, 179). New research on the effects of early childhood music instruction will result in greater efforts at educating all ages, from early childhood through adulthood. Music teachers may also become partners with community organizations which will require some flexibility in terms of music class schedules and venues.

Future Education Reforms

This chapter raises many questions and makes predictions about the future of music education. Some will result in education reforms, and because many readers of this book will become leaders in music education, the following points are important to keep in mind about reform (Boston 1996):

- It must be systemic and holistic, not fragmented.
- The principal and superintendent are main forces in school reform.
- The parents must be involved.
- The taxpayers must be supportive.
- High standards and high expectations are required.

Why Teach?

Finally, the question of why we want to be teachers is the quintessential one. As we consider the life of an educator, we know that it is one of continual intellectual and creative growth. Our lives will be full of the art of music, and we will have control over the quality of that music. We will experience continual personal growth as we work to serve as ethical role models for our students. It is a satisfying career for these reasons.

But more importantly, our purpose as music educators is to equip young people with the capacity to experience, discover and create beauty in a world that desperately needs it. No one says it will be easy. But the positive influence of music teachers will be remembered by their students for a lifetime (see Appendix).

Once again, the college student preparing to become a music educator should ask: **Why is music education so important that I want to spend my entire professional life in it?**

Questions, Topics and Activities for Critical Thinking

1. Discuss how you see the role of music education in fulfilling the four outcomes of the Framework for 21st Century Learning.
2. Discuss your hopes, concerns and predictions for the future of music education.
3. Explore the websites for the Partnership for 21st Century Skills and for the Arts Education Partnership for ways to become involved in the future of arts education.
4. Explore an aspect of technology that you have never used, write a three-page paper on its use, and demonstrate it to the class.
5. Review your previously written philosophy of music education, and update it according to the new knowledge you have acquired this semester.

Readings

Arts Education Partnership, www.ccsso.org/projects/arts_education_partnership/ (retrieved 3/14/09).

Baskerville, David (2006). *Music Business Handbook and Career Guide*, 8th ed. Thousand Oaks, CA: Sage Publications.

Boston, Bruce O. (1996). "Education Reform? No Mysteries." In *Aiming for Excellence: The Impact of the Standards Movement on Music Education*. Reston, VA: MENC.

Brown, Andrew R. & Steven Dillon (2007). "Networked Improvisational Musical Environments: Learning Through On-line Collaborative Music Making." In John Finney & Pamela Burnard (eds.), *Music Education with Digital Technology* (pp. 95–106). London: Continuum International Publishing Group.

Conway, Colleen M. & Thomas M. Hodgman (2009). *Teaching Music in Higher Education*. New York: Oxford.

Deturk, Mark S. (2002). "Critical and Creative Thinking." In Eunice Boardman (ed.), *Dimensions of Musical Learning and Teaching: A Different Kind of Classroom*. Reston, VA: MENC.

Fowler, Charles (1996). *Strong Arts, Strong Schools: The Promising Potential and Shortsighted Disregard of the Arts in American Schooling*, 105. New York: Oxford.

Hill, Douglas (February 2003). "Occupation Hazard: Is Your Job Damaging Your Hearing?" *Teaching Music*, 36–40.

Hodges, Richard (2007). "Music Education and Training: ICT, Innovation and Curriculum Reform." In John Finney & Pamela Burnard (eds.), *Music Education with Digital Technology* (pp. 169–180). London: Continuum International Publishing Group.

Jellison, Judith A. (2000). "How Can All People Continue to be Involved in Meaningful Music Participation?" In Clifford K. Madsen (ed.), *Vision 2020: The Housewright Symposium on the Future of Music Education* (pp. 111–137). Reston, VA: MENC.

Koopman, Constantijn (2005). "Music Education, Performativity and Aestheticization." In David K. Lines (ed.), *Music Education for the New Millennium: Theory and Practice Futures for Music Teaching and Learning*. Malden, MA: Blackwell Publishing.

Lamont, A., D.J. Hargreaves, A. Marshall & M. Tarrant (2003). "Young People's Music In and Out of School." *British Journal of Music Education, 20*(3), 229–241.

Leong, Samuel (2007). "Strategies for Enabling Curriculum Reform: Lessons from Australia, Singapore and Hong Kong." In John Finney & Pamela Burnard (eds.), *Music Education with Digital Technology* (pp. 181–195). London: Continuum International Publishing Group.

Lines, David K. (2005). "Improvisation and Cultural Work in Music and Music Education." In David K. Lines (ed.), *Music Education for the New Millennium: Theory and Practice Futures for Music Teaching and Learning*. Malden, MA: Blackwell Publishing.

Madura Ward-Steinman, P. (Spring, 2007). "Confidence in Teaching Improvisation According to the K–12 Achievement Standards: Surveys of Vocal Jazz Workshop Participants and Undergraduates." *Bulletin of the Council for Research in Music Education, 172*, 25–40.

Medical Problems of Performing Artists (1986–2009), 1–24.

Nardo, Rachel (2009). "See! Hear! Enhanced Podcasting with GarageBand." *General Music Today, 23(1)*, 27–30.

Partnership for 21st Century Skills (2007). Available www.21stcenturyskills.org.

Regelski, Thomas A. (2005). "Music and Music Education: Theory and Praxis for 'Making a Difference.'" In David K. Lines (ed.), *Music Education for the New Millennium: Theory and Practice Futures for Music Teaching and Learning*. Malden, MA: Blackwell Publishing.

Robinson, Kenneth (2006). Available http://www.ted.com/index.php/talks/view/id/66.

Ruthmann, S. Alex (2007). "Strategies for Supporting Music Learning Through On-line Collaborative Technologies." In John Finney & Pamela Burnard (eds.), *Music Education with Digital Technology* (pp. 131–141). London: Continuum International Publishing Group.

Spearman, Carlesta Elliott (2000). "How Will Societal and Technological Change Affect the Teaching of Music?" In Clifford K. Madsen (ed.), *Vision 2020: The Housewright Symposium on the Future of Music Education* (pp. 155–184). Reston, VA: MENC.

appendix
The Power of Music Education

Two True Stories

James Quinn[1]

After graduating from the United States Naval Academy, Jim Quinn became a Naval aviator, flying hundreds of combat missions and making over 200 carrier landings. After retiring from the Navy, he worked on the research staff of the Center for Naval Analyses. He is now a Certified Financial Planner. Music has played a large part in his life, and it is a testament to the power of music education that he considers his seventh grade choral music teacher to be the most influential teacher of his life. The following is from Mr. Quinn's unpublished memoir.

Certainly the highlight of 7th grade was my introduction to music. "Mr. G," as we affectionately knew the music teacher, certainly was the most influential teacher, if not person, I experienced in my life. He had been in the Army in the war and came back to Park High, reclaiming his job as choral music teacher, something that veterans were able to do, from a man who went elsewhere to places unknown. His only known claim to fame was that he had christened the Glee Club "The Oriolions" (our athletic teams were the St. Louis Park Orioles), a name which Mr. G instantly discarded in favor of, simply, "The St. Louis Park High School Glee Club."

But the Glee Club was in the future for us 7th graders. We had art three times per week, and music twice the first semester, swapping that schedule in semester two. And here we simply started singing out of, as I recall, a book of songs, which could well have been a hymn book in those days. In the second semester, Mr. G formed an extracurricular choral group of 7th grade girls, to sing just for fun, not inviting the boys whom he found too boisterous. This bugged me, and I was a regular onlooker, sitting in the back of the music room while the girls rehearsed. Finally one day, seeing that I was pretty serious in my interest, Mr. G said "Won't you join us?" which I eagerly did. This was, of course, outrageous favoritism shown towards me, and my buddy Brian Olson got wind of it and immediately protested, "If Quinn can do this, why can't we?" It did him no good, and I remained the favored one.

The real reinforcement of this attachment to music began with Mr. G, probably going into high gear with entry into the Junior High Chorus in 8th grade. The chorus was the feeder to the Glee Club and the Girl's Chorus (for those senior high girls whose voices weren't good enough for the 100-person Glee Club). Our chorus room was well laid out, five rows of 20 seats each, aisles separating five seats at either end from the main section, with the end sections angled in towards the center to form a semicircular effect.

Mr. G divided the year into four units of nine-weeks' duration each. After an initial grounding in reading key signatures and getting our do-re-mes down pat, he would train our ears by playing notes on the piano while we wrote the notes on music paper. He would do somewhat the same thing by playing notes in various rhythms, and we would transcribe the whole notes, ½ notes, c notes, etc. onto paper. We then learned the musical language: *adagio, allegro, allegretto, vivace, poco a poco,* etc., so that we could understand and follow the dynamic markings of what we were singing. We learned the sounds of the instruments of the orchestra as he played records of solo instruments that he called on us to identify. And he would bring new gadgets into class to experiment with—early tape recorders, a wire recorder. This went on through the two years of Junior High Chorus, at the end of which I could read music fairly well, a skill that helped me through another 40-plus years of choral singing.

The most traumatic thing he required was for each of us to do "a talent," i.e., he required each of us to do a solo performance in front of the entire class. For those studying an instrument or piano and who were used to recitals, this was no big thing. For the rest of us, singing was the only option, and we were generally terrified. We could do duets, so I took the hymn *Joshua Fit the Battle of Jericho,* harmonized it (alas, not very well) for two male voices and got Paul Herman to join me as "da walls come a tumbelin' down." We got through it.

Mr. G managed our trips to the young people's concerts of the Minneapolis Symphony, keeping a wary eye out for any miscreants who got out of line during the performances. And he was very specific about binoculars and opera glasses: "We don't use those in our section," he would admonish us. He wanted us to appreciate classical music, so he would beforehand play excerpts of pieces we would hear at upcoming concerts. Or he would have Jackie Hjermstad play something the soloist, e.g., Claudio Arrau, planned to play. The concerts themselves were, of course, quite wonderful, and we were privileged to hear musical greats of the day with the fine Minneapolis Symphony conducted by Dimitri Mitropoulos (who left Minneapolis about 1950 to take over the New York Philharmonic), followed by Antal Dorati. (My mom was a member of the Women's Association of the Minneapolis Symphony: "Oh, he's so handsome!")

Rudolph Serkin, the great pianist, played one of the youth concerts, and Paul Herman and I were rather stunned to count at least eight obvious wrong notes he played in a Chopin piece we knew. Mr. G said we were being too harsh—it was tough playing before that youth audience (lots of chatter), and the concert would have been low on his priority list. It still shattered our illusions about famous musicians not ever making mistakes—they are human, and they get stage fright, as we now all know.

Mr. G was not a musical snob—he enjoyed popular as well as classical music, as we shall see a little later. He spoke very approvingly of singers like Bing Crosby and Frank

Sinatra, saying that even though they didn't have great classical voices, they used the voices they had very, very well.

Glee Club

The teaching of music fundamentals was now over, and we concentrated on singing in the senior Glee Club class, which was the last period of the day, just a nice time to enjoy singing, and no homework. I think we anticipated singing an hour a day, five days per week, with some anxiety—wouldn't that get ... boring? No, it was wonderful.

Fundamental to our success as a chorus was the weekly sectional rehearsal, held from 8:00 a.m. to 8:25 a.m. each of four mornings during the week, with one of the four voice sections attending each rehearsal. Your grade for each marking period was determined solely by attendance at sectionals—perfect attendance resulted in an "A." If a singer missed too many sectionals—out!

I sang in a number of choral groups during my life, but I've always believed the St. Louis Park High School Glee Club to be technically the best. Except for oratorios, we memorized all our music, and we knew the notes and rhythms perfectly. We gave about ten performances each year, most of the music sung a cappella, formal concerts as well as singing for groups having particular events. And we sang everything from Bach and Brahms to the music of Fred Waring and the Pennsylvanians, which Mr. G seemed to truly enjoy, and of course the kids did, too.

But the best was the sacred music, which formed the major portion of our repertoire. I suppose it would be impossible to sing that music in a secondary school today. Particularly beautiful pieces were Brahms' *How Lovely Is Thy Dwelling Place* from *Requiem*, an especially fine setting of the 23rd Psalm, James Macbeth's *Brother James Air*; and *Jesu Mein Freude (Jesus, Dearest Master)* of Bach. We also sang Theodore DuBois' *Seven Last Words of Christ*, an Easter Oratorio. Another favorite was *Carousel*, all that wonderful music from the Broadway show. "We had a real nice clambake, we're mighty glad we came, the victuals we ate were good, you bet ... " still echoes in my mind.

The Glee Club sang the Christmas portion of Handel's *Messiah*, which I particularly loved, every other year and I was just sorry that the timing was such that I only got to sing it my junior year. For Christmas in the late 1940s, Mom had given me a complete recording of *Messiah*, performed by the Huddersfield Choral Society. I "found" it even before Christmas that year and merrily played it anytime she was away in those weeks before Christmas. It was an open secret that I would get it, and one day she said, "I suppose you've played it already!" Apparently I had not covered my tracks well.

For Christmas, 1952 Antal Dorati would conduct *Messiah* with the Minneapolis Symphony, and he planned to enlist all the Minneapolis high school choirs (Mr. G accurately classified us as a glee club; in Minneapolis the directors mostly inaccurately classified their groups as choirs, which he defined to be a "church chorus"), about 1,000 singers, to do *Messiah* with the symphony. One day Mr. G announced that (somehow) he had gotten us included in the cast of a thousand. Heady stuff, we were quite thrilled. But a few weeks later he announced the deal was off, we would do our own.

Thinking of 1,000 teenagers singing the runs in *For Unto Us a Child Is Born* or *His Yoke is Easy, His Burthen Is Light* makes one shudder, and I think we were well out of it. We sang 12 choruses from parts I and II, and did a beautiful job. One of the highlights was Mr. G himself, with his fine, lyrical tenor voice, leading off with *Comfort Ye My People* and *Every Valley Shall Be Exalted*.

St. Louis Park was in the Lake Conference for athletics, and there was an annual get-together of the Glee Clubs from the seven schools in the conference, where we all gave short performances. We were clearly the best of the lot, and I remember the admiring faces of members of the other choruses in the audience as we performed.

Rebecca J. Cohen, MD[2]

Rebecca J. Cohen, MD, is a graduate of the Mt. Sinai School of Medicine, and completed residency training at Montefiore Medical Center in Bronx, New York, where she served as chief resident of the Internal Medicine-Primary Care/Social Medicine Program. Dr. Cohen is board certified in internal medicine and specializes in comprehensive care, managing both common and complex illness in adults and adolescents, yet keeps active as a flutist and credits her music teachers for their strong influence on her life. The following is from an interview with Dr. Cohen, conducted by Patrice Madura on May 18, 2009.

I started playing the flute the summer before 4th grade in a public school in New Jersey. I started in a summer workshop and it took me a good part of the summer just to get a sound out of it, but I stuck with it. I always looked forward to band in 4th and 5th grade. By middle school I became involved in regional band competitions, played in the school jazz band and in small ensembles like flute trios and quartets.

My best friend played the flute too so we played flute duets all the time. I had a good rapport with our middle school band teacher. He was young and I think he took a liking to us because we hung around the band room, always knew the music and practiced a lot. And then he definitely showed that he took an interest because he gave my brother and me (my brother played the clarinet) the opportunity to play with the Jersey City State Wind Ensemble, a college group. In fact, he used to pick us up and drive us to Jersey City which was about 30 minutes away! I think that was really going above and beyond. And that was a great experience because it was a lot more challenging music than what we got at the middle school level. It was a good opportunity to play with people at a higher level consistently. I was also able to perform a concertino with the group. I held a special place for the teacher that gave me that opportunity. I think he really cared about the students.

He also organized the end of the year ensembles concert which to me was a big deal. There was an outdoor concert for which I could play in a flute quartet and also a solo piece that my brother would accompany on the piano. Our jazz band did lots of competitions. As a flute player in a jazz band you get to play a little solo so that you can be heard. Once or twice we went to Hershey Park in the spring for a competition. My life in and out of school really revolved around music. I always did well academically but the thing I enjoyed and craved the most were the band rehearsals and other musical opportunities. That's what I enjoyed so much.

I think I have a competitive side to me, and I enjoyed that I really excelled at flute. I was especially driven by my private flute teacher. I studied at a local music center through the middle of 7th grade, and then switched to this teacher who told me that I would have to practice for an hour a day if I wanted to study with her. That was fine with me, and it was then that I started to be more and more driven. I believed—and this is just my personality—I'm very methodical—that if I practiced and worked hard at it then I would get good at it. And it worked. I got better and better, and then I got a new flute at the end of 7th grade which took me up another notch. It was just gratifying. I think it was also around that time that I got to see James Galway in concert—it was an incredible experience. I actually got his autograph during intermission, something I still treasure. I also realized meeting him that he is relatively short in stature (as I am)! In 8th grade I had to get braces—I cried that night when I practiced and realized how much harder it was. It made for a tough 11 months but I think I came out a stronger player in the long run.

My high school had a big music program with good funding. I knew the ropes about the program because my brother was a year older and very involved as well. I got my braces off in late September which was a thrilling occasion, mainly because my tone improved so much overnight. The region band auditions were in December, and even as a freshman I came in first, which was really shocking to me. I wasn't expecting that at all—I was just hoping to get in. I'll always remember the phone call that night. My brother was the one on the phone with our choir teacher, and he kept holding up one finger showing I'd come in first; but I didn't understand what he was gesturing for what seemed like a long time!

I also joined the high school marching band and jazz band, and I always had a lot of respect for our teacher and really looked up to him. I generally really enjoyed marching band. The whole Fall centered around it. I got to play piccolo solos. I played in the elementary jazz band my first year and then got into the top jazz band which did well in state and national competitions. I had a lot of really tough solos with lots and lots of notes, and some slower ones too, and came home with several best soloist trophies. That was a big thing for me that I was given that experience.

My private teacher was very rigid when it came to mastering technique and insisted on practicing really slowly and moving the metronome up one notch at a time. I'm good at following directions in that very methodical way so we worked well together. I think that the school program provided the atmosphere for my competitive drive to come out. I know that the social environment and the competitive environment were what I was really thriving on. And those were provided by the teachers for sure. Socially, we were all together from 7:00 to 8:00 a.m. every morning for marching band rehearsal and then on the weekend we'd go to all of the football games and competitions. Life revolved around it. And for better or for worse, and I know there is some worse in there, the music program was centered on competitions. Marching band and jazz band competition. Region competition. All-state competition. But I am a competitive person so I loved it.

I also went to music camp at a college for several summers during high school. My best friend went too. We stayed in the dorms. That experience was just incredible to me. There you were exposed to fine conductors from around the country. I played in the wind ensemble and also the orchestra which I hadn't really done much of at all. The region orchestra was the only orchestra I'd ever played in. This gave me a chance to play with only one flute player on a part. One of the counselors there was one of the flutists. She was studying at Eastman and was phenomenal and I considered her sort of a mentor. There was a one- to two-week block where she was the principal and I was the second flutist. I loved the music and it felt really special. And there was a campwide choir that all these great musicians sang in together. I also took conducting and theory classes there, and the conductors were of the caliber of what you'd get at the all-state and region level.

My parents fully supported all of these musical opportunities and got a lot of vicarious pleasure from seeing my brother and me pursue music in ways they hadn't been able to do growing up. Yet they were clear they didn't want us to pursue music professionally. My brother also went to medical school and after a year he dropped out and became a choral conductor. He got a DMA and is teaching at a high school in Connecticut. And he's really happy. I'm comfortable with my decision to keep music as an avocation. Medicine always grabbed me. One of the reasons I picked Columbia College was because I could major in pre-med and still do a concentration in music. I ended up having a flute teacher there who was a member of the New York Philharmonic and it was another great opportunity to study with a renowned teacher.

I think there is a connection between medicine and music. You need to have a lot of perseverance and drive to pursue medicine; there is a parallel in music because you can't become a great musician overnight. It is a very different outlet for sure. However, I'd rather be known as someone who plays the flute rather than just a doctor. I appreciate the musical sense in me more in a way. I don't know what the exact link is but I know I wrote in my medical school application essay that my ideal goal was to be a physician who played in a doctor's orchestra on the side. It was always part of my plan.

One of the best classes in all of college was a music history course because of the professor. It was the passion that he showed. You could sometimes see that passion in a professor of math or science, but those subjects were relatively dry. This professor was really excited about his topic, Czech music. And the course was very organized—I guess I like organization. I loved the music but especially the way he brought it to life. For me, after all of these science classes and then to go to this class at 9 in the morning where the professor would do a kind of impromptu in the middle of the lecture—just singing in this beautiful tenor voice while playing the piano excerpt from one of the pieces that we were studying—that was really magical and it really inspired me and my interest in the material.

The other major performance that stands out for me was in my senior year in college, during the same semester as the music history course just described. I was one of the winners of the concerto competition at Columbia. It was super-challenging and I practiced all summer—I had auditions for the concerto competition the year before and didn't do so well, but every year I had made a real leap. In my freshman year I didn't get into the college orchestra which was demoralizing after going to this very competitive high school where I'd excelled. It was hard. But by my senior year I really worked my way up and this was the crowning experience. I played the most challenging piece I'd ever played, and from memory. It was, at least thus far, the height of my musical life.

Later, in medical school, I kept performing by seeking out other musicians to play with. There was a pianist and a violist who were a year ahead of me. When a coffee house performance would come up 2–3 times a year we would put something together. By my 3rd or 4th year, one of the 1st year med students was a great violinist, so there were enough musicians trickling in that there was always someone to play with.

Then I went to my medical residency, an Internal Medicine program focusing on Primary Care and Social medicine. I found all these very artsy people whose interests went far beyond just medicine. While I was there I found a great cellist to play with, and we joined forces with the violist and violinist from Mt. Sinai to perform. We played string quartets with me on the first violin part. We did a couple of concerts a year. Not a lot, but enough.

I've been practicing internal medicine here since 2006. After my daughter was born in 2006, I didn't play very much for two years (except nursery rhyme tunes) and I was really worried I wouldn't get it back. Then last summer I realized that she was old enough that I could go out and play in a group. So I joined the community band over the summer and did a few concerts with them. Their motto is not to be competitive which doesn't quite fit with my personality but it was the perfect way back into playing and they were quite welcoming. It was hard to find the time but I started playing with my synagogue once a month. Someone there asked me if I'd heard of the Southern Indiana Wind Ensemble, and so I emailed the conductor that night. It turned out that they were having auditions that weekend. Once again that really brought out my competitive drive and I thought "I can do this." I practiced when my daughter was napping and I got into the group. So this year has given me music back. Since college what I've learned is that to get all that musicality I have to draw it out of myself, and draw on what I learned from all of my teachers over the years. That's part of growing up I guess.

I think the impact of music education is huge. Even though I was lucky in that I succeeded academically, what I really enjoyed in grades 4–12 was music. I was not particularly athletic so gym class or extracurricular athletics were never my strong suit. I felt so comfortable with music and it gave me a lot of opportunity to shine in a way that I liked shining. My private teacher was key—she was the outside force that allowed me to develop my technique and musicality—but then I got to show it off at school. That was the medium for me. I don't do well when there's no group to play with. It's when I find other people to play with that I really thrive. And I am still very close to my best friend with whom I've played flute duets since 6th grade!

Notes

Chapter 3

1. www.oake.org.
2. www.aosa.org.
3. www.dalcrozeusa.org.
4. www.scottforesman.com.
5. www.isimprov.org.
6. www.music.org/atmi.
7. http://boethius.music.ucsb.edu/smt-list/smthome.html.
8. www.music.org.

Chapter 6

1. One of the few things that music education professional associations do not do is certify, or license, music teachers. In some professions, medicine, for instance, the states license them to practice after their professional associations certify them as being prepared to practice their specialties. Since teacher certification is a function of state government, each state department of education is responsible for granting teachers the right to teach in its public schools.
2. The Special Research Interest Groups are Adult and Community Music Education; Affective Response; Assessment; Children with Exceptionalities; Creativity; Early Childhood; Gender Research in Music Education; History; Instructional Strategies; Learning and Development; Music Teacher Education; Perception and Cognition; Philosophy; and Social Sciences.

Chapter 10

1. Hazel Nohavec Morgan, ed., *Music Education Source Book* (Chicago, IL: Music Educators National Conference, 1947), xi–xii.
2. From Robert Choate, ed., *Documentary Report of the Tanglewood Symposium* (Washington, DC: Music Educators National Conference, 1968), 138–139.
3. National Commission on Music Education, "Education with Music," *Growing Up Complete: The Imperative for Music Education* (Reston, VA: MENC, 1991), 17–18.

4. Music Educators National Conference. 1806 Robert Fulton Dr., Reston, VA 22091 Copyright © 1994.

5. The Housewright Declaration. *Vision 2020: The Housewright Symposium on the Future of Music Education* (Reston, VA: Music Educators National Conference: The National Association for Music Education, 2000, 219–220. Copyright © Music Educators National Conference: The National Association for Music Education).

6. From *Music Education at a Crossroads: Realizing the Goal of Music for All,* edited by Janet R. Barrett. Copyright © 2009 by MENC: The National Association for Music Education. Used with permission.

Appendix

1. Printed by permission of James Quinn.
2. Printed by permission of Rebecca J. Cohen.

Index